DEPARTMENT OF THE ENVIRONMENT

Transforming our Waste Land: The Way Forward

UNIVERSITY OF LIVERPOOL
ENVIRONMENTAL ADVISORY UNIT

LONDON
HER MAJESTY'S STATIONERY OFFICE

HMSO BOOKS

HMSO publications are available from:

HMSO Publications Centre
(Mail and telephone orders only)
PO Box 276, London SW8 5DT
Telephone orders (01) 622 3316
General enquiries (01) 211 5656

HMSO Bookshops
49 High Holborn, London, WC1V 6HB   (01) 211 5656 (Counter service only)
258 Broad Street, Birmingham, B1 2HE   (021) 643 3757
Southey House, 33 Wine Street, Bristol, BS1 2BQ   (0272) 24306/24307
9-21 Princess Street, Manchester, M60 8AS   (061) 834 7201
80 Chichester Street, Belfast, BT1 4JY   (0232) 234488
13a Castle Street, Edinburgh, EH2 3AR   (031) 225 6333

HMSO's Accredited Agents
(see Yellow Pages)

and through good booksellers

CoC.B 43311/9.95. 9.89

ISBN 0 11 751810 7

Foreword

I am very pleased to be able to welcome the publication of *Transforming our Waste Land – The Way Forward*. I am sure that it will be read by a wide range of people who can help to achieve the results we all want to see.

The Department of the Environment attaches particular importance to clearing past dereliction and to avoiding its creation in the future by reclaiming and recycling damaged land. My Department has an important part to play at the national level in achieving these aims. But others in the minerals, waste disposal and construction industries; local authorities; business; nature conservation, sporting and leisure interests and voluntary organisations also have a direct and vital part to play.

This report by the University of Liverpool's Environmental Advisory Unit, with its illustrated case studies, should stimulate and broaden the ideas of those already undertaking land reclamation and provide an impetus for new initiative from others. I commend it to you.

SIR GEORGE YOUNG Bt MP

Contents

Introduction

In Britain we have a serious problem concerning our land. It is a problem of wasted land, land which is derelict, degraded and neglected. It is a problem which stems from our industrial past, when land was used to feed the demands of industry without any thought for the future. It is a problem of the present also, because the demands of industry still have to be satisfied, and new houses, roads and factories must be built.

We use land for many different purposes. At some time or other the same land becomes disused, for instance when mines or gravel pits are worked out, when factories become obsolete, or when houses are too old to provide modern standards of comfort and convenience.

If land was immediately put back to its original use, such as the agriculture before it was mined, or put to some new use, such as a public park after the houses are removed, there would be no problem. The land would be re-used and recycled like any other material.

If land is left degraded, with only the tattered remnants of its former use to proclaim its past, we are guilty of two major transgressions. Firstly, that a valuable resource is being wasted, and secondly, that our environment and that of our children is being eroded.

This book discusses what has happened, what is happening, and what we can do about it. Like solving any problem, the solution is in part technical. But perhaps more than anything else it is a matter of imagination and determination. As evidence of this, there are excellent examples of these qualities being used in practice, some of which are described in succeeding pages.

The book does not provide all the answers. Some of them are matters of new policy and new approaches by government, local authorities, industry and the general public. But we hope that enough is shown to indicate that the problem is not insoluble.

Alison Burt
Anthony Bradshaw

University of Liverpool
Environmental Advisory Unit
July 1985

Chapter 1

The Inheritance

1.1 Waste land

The first step in any problem is to make quite clear what is being talked about. So what is this wasted land? It comes in all sorts of shapes and sizes and can be described in all sorts of different ways. Indeed, many words have been used, such as derelict, degraded, devastated, destroyed, neglected. Many of these words have come to have special meanings in official usage. For our purposes we need a 'blanket' term for all these different sorts. They can all be best described as 'waste land'.

Waste land – any land which because of neglect or degradation is not being used to its full potential. It is composed of:

(a) *Derelict land* – land which has been so damaged by industrial and other development that it is incapable of beneficial use without treatment.

(b) *Neglected land* – land which though capable of some beneficial use is at present uncared for, untidy and in a condition detrimental to the environment.

(c) *Operational land* – those parts of land within a current development which are not realising their full potential and are detrimental to the environment.

These three components of waste land are, of course, not tidily separate from one another; they intergrade. But the essential point is that in each the land is wasted and could be used in a better way.

Waste land is, or can be, a very negative part of our environment as an eyesore, misery or threat. An untreated urban clearance area is an eyesore to those who pass by, it is a misery to the children for whom it is their only playground, and it is a threat as a supply of bricks and stones which can be thrown at windows. An untreated mine site is the same, but the Aberfan disaster will remind us of the size of the threat.

Land is our most precious inheritance. It is vital to our existence. We grow crops for food on it, we construct houses for shelter on it and we

Figure 1.1 Part of our waste land inheritance – an urban clearance area.

mine its resources. It is imperative that it is managed properly. Yet land is abused continually. Unfortunately, the full implication of this has not been realised by previous generations and we have inherited an appalling legacy of dereliction and neglect. It is of prime importance that we understand what contributes to waste land and what is its nature and scale. Only then can we work towards its remedy.

1.2 The different sorts of waste land

(a) Derelict land
The waste land which troubles us most is derelict land, because it is the most difficult to deal with. Because of past activities on the site, the original land surface has been completely destroyed or buried, or thoroughly degraded – perhaps by some toxic waste. Disused buildings are just as much a cause of land becoming derelict as waste heaps. As a result there are many different kinds of derelict land.

Spoil heaps consisting of the wastes from coal and other mining operations are very obvious to the general public. The materials are raw and may be so toxic that nothing will grow on them. They are sufficiently unstable that they cannot be built on. They are a gaunt reminder of the past. In the same neighbourhood, there is often another result of the mining activity, underground collapse, leading to subsidence at the surface and sometimes flooded areas – mining flashes.

Excavations and pits have been left by the extraction of limestone and chalk for agriculture, building and chemicals, sand and gravel for cement and concrete, and clay for bricks. Some of these pits are enormous, many acres in extent, others are quite small. Many low lying pits have become filled with water and are now lakes and marshes.

Derelict military installations form another major category. They are usually extensive sites scattered with the remains of buildings and roads,

Figure 1.3   An inheritance we can do without; derelict land in St Helens.

sometimes with toxic areas within them. However, some of the original land surface may remain.

Derelict railway land is the price we pay for the great extension of our use of motor vehicles. Some of it can be remarkably beautiful, but much of it is dismal ballast-covered areas behind the back streets of cities.

The other forms of derelict land are those due predominantly to industrial and urban decline and change. They include old gasworks sites, disused docks and factories, and some urban housing clearance areas. The essential characteristic of all these sites is their mess and complexity due to the remains of old buildings and other structures, making new development very difficult. There may be some toxicity, as in gasworks sites, due to past chemical processes.

Figure 1.4 Some derelict land is an inevitable result of change; there are over 8,000 hectares of derelict railway land.

(b) Neglected and other land

Perhaps the most obviously neglected areas are the areas of once agricultural land on the urban fringe awaiting development to housing or factories. The development may have started, the roads laid, and one or two factories built. The rest remains as a disorganised wilderness attracting illicit rubbish dumping. These areas may consist of just a small undeveloped site intended for a single factory, or be part of a well established housing estate intended for some purpose that was never fulfilled. But often we are dealing with agricultural land which has been neglected on purpose, in the hope that it will be recognised as ripe for industrial development.

Derelict land itself often has neglected land associated which is potentially good land but is not used due to problems of ownership and the proximity of the derelict area.

The disappearance of a previous land use without any defined new use can cause neglect; for instance, old woodland areas can become too small to be economic or small agricultural areas can be left over when most of a holding was sold. Some of this is the result of some planned development

Figure 1.5 'Interim' sites in cities waiting for redevelopment can have a depressing effect on their surroundings.

such as a road or an airport and has the delightful term SLOAP – space left over after planning. There are various sorts of land which have uses, supposedly, but the sites have either never been properly developed for them or they have just become wasted. Terrible examples of the former are refuse disposal sites intended for public open space but never finished properly. The latter can include old cemeteries and even some public open space. Regrettably there is even derelict land which has been reclaimed under a previous scheme, such as Operation Eyesore, and then just left because there was no money to maintain it.

Finally, there is another type of site which, unfortunately, people in responsible positions often do not attend to. These are the multitude of sites within cities which are going to be developed soon. But, alas, some of these 'interim' lands have a habit of remaining undeveloped for several years, casting a blight on their surroundings.

(c) Operational land
Many people will think it is improper to include any part of operational land in waste land, because by definition, operational land is wanted for operations. Yet in some cases it has to be recognised that some operational land must be counted as waste land. In large scale mining operations there can be parts of a site, often at the periphery, which are not being used and are unlikely to be used for a long time. These can cast a great and unnecessary blight on the surrounding land. The blight is unnecessary because the land could be treated in some simple temporary way to improve it. If it really is not wanted, it could even be restored to grassland and let out on an annual grazing licence to a neighbouring farmer.

1.3 How much?

Once the different sorts are listed it is not difficult to see that the total amount might be quite considerable. If we take first the land which is officially recognised as derelict, the best available estimate for England, Wales and Scotland is 71,155 hectares (over 175,000 acres) based on Government surveys about 1974. This represents an area greater than the whole of Merseyside. For England, the most recent survey records 45,700ha in 1982. But what is crucial is that the previous survey, eight years before, recorded 43,300ha of derelict land in England. The amount of derelict land has, therefore, been increasing despite greater efforts at restoration. Although some of the observed increase may be due to

improved recording methods, this is a depressing state of affairs.

But there is also all the other waste land as well. If this is added, the estimates for the total amount of waste land in England give an even more depressing picture. A careful survey has suggested that in 1974, the total for England was 200,000ha, an area equal to the whole of West Sussex. In fact, the ratio of the area of waste to derelict land is about 3½:1. Neglected and other land is therefore a serious element in our problem, although it can often be returned to productive use at comparatively low cost.

Besides all this there is current operational land and land for which permission for working has been obtained but has not yet commenced. This constitutes roughly another 123,000 hectares. A large part of this is working and is certainly not wasteland. But parts of it are lying idle, and, taken as a whole, operational land does have an impact, so we must consider it.

1.4 Where?

Waste land is everyone's problem and some peoples' special problem. Although it is ubiquitous, it is also unevenly distributed over the nation. It is certainly not confined to industrial areas but occurs in rural locations, National Parks and Areas of Outstanding Natural Beauty.

In 1982, there were 24,680ha of derelict land in rural areas compared with 21,000ha in urban areas. Nevertheless, there is a marked concentration in places associated with coal, iron, steel and chemical industries, particularly where these industries have subsequently declined or moved to newer industrial districts.

As a result, the amount of dereliction does vary considerably between counties (see Figure 1.7). Cornwall has the largest amount of derelict land because of its inherited dereliction from old workings – particularly former metalliferous mining. If the figures for land restoration are taken into account, then Greater Manchester, with a much better record than Cornwall on reclamation, has actually contained a higher total acreage of derelict land over the years 1974-82 (Table 1.1). Much of the dereliction in Greater Manchester comes from decline in factories and housing. Other more rural areas, such as Northumberland and Cumbria, have disturbing amounts of dereliction.

Not only does the amount of derelict land differ between counties but also the type of derelict land (Table 1.2). Spoil heaps form the largest single category of derelict land in England, followed by 'other forms'.

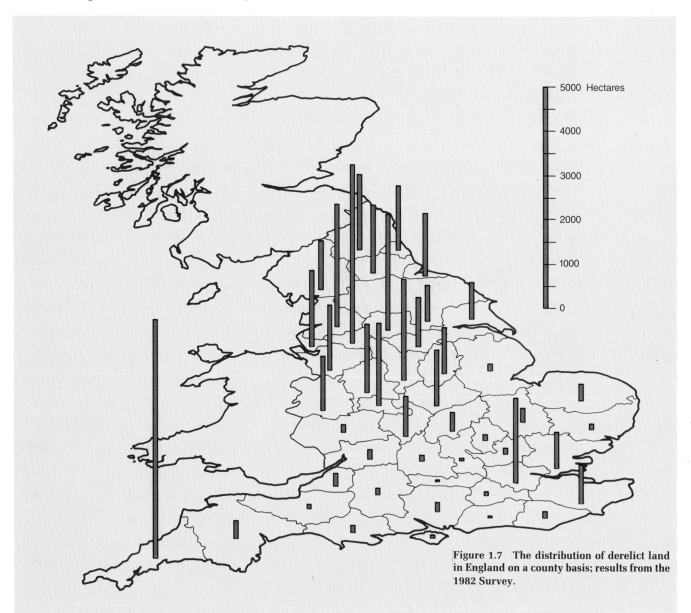

Figure 1.7   The distribution of derelict land in England on a county basis; results from the 1982 Survey.

Table 1.1 **The amount of derelict and restored land in selected counties in England from 1974 to 1982**

County	Derelict land (hectares)		Restored (hectares) 1974-1982
	1974	1982	
Cornwall	4574	5384	131
Greater Manchester	3405	4035	1727
Lancashire	2470	2742	613
Northumberland	2411	1735	658
Cumbria	1733	1105	282
Greater London	324	1954	422
West Sussex	0	14	90
Berkshire	21	6	22
Total for England	43273	45683	16952

Table 1.2 **The distribution of different categories of derelict land in England in 1982**

Region	Spoil heaps	Excavation and pits	Military etc. dereliction	Derelict railway land	Other forms of dereliction	Total
North	1872	1043	168	1375	2849	7307
North West	2012	1381	398	1648	4603	10042
Yorkshire & Humberside	1070	1433	385	1428	1115	5431
West Midlands	2174	917	330	875	1491	5787
East Midlands	1225	1258	644	1339	732	5198
East Anglia	15	305	251	170	63	804
South West	4870	420	208	820	317	6635
South East (ex. G.L.)	57	1439	268	374	387	2525
Greater London	45	382	364	181	982	1954
Total for England	13340	8578	3016	8210	12539	45683

These other forms of dereliction, such as disused gas works, factories etc. account for nearly 50% of derelict land in the North West, which has the largest overall area of dereliction in the country. Excavations and derelict railways form roughly equal areas, but both types of dereliction are more prevalent in the north.

These categories are easily identified and their origin is clear. There nevertheless remains the much larger amount of waste land which is less easily defined and is poorly recorded, and which arises from a variety of causes. This land is particularly associated with urban fringes, abandoned allotments, neglected public open space, demolition sites, disused industrial installations and derelict buildings, most of it obvious to the general public. Because of uncertainties of ownership and plans for development, many of these sites may remain unused for many years.

Finally, there is the operational land which occurs, in particular, wherever there is mining. It is associated with suitable hard rocks, such as limestone in Derbyshire, with sand and gravel deposits in the Home Counties, with special deposits such as china clay and tin in Cornwall, and with the coalfields. So these areas are scattered, but in many cases they are close to the towns and villages which have grown up in association with them. Any impact caused by operational land is therefore likely to be important.

1.5 The effects of waste land

Land degradation can have complex and far-reaching effects not confined to the waste land itself but extending over a much larger area. The material that blows from spoil heaps can give rise to dust in the air which may persist long after the production of spoil has ceased and can cause permanent contamination. There can be wholesale movement, as happened in the Aberfan disaster in 1966, although hopefully this will never occur again. Old mine workings can produce large quantities of drainage water, containing toxic substances such as lead and zinc, or acids in solution, which pollute streams, rivers and lakes.

The great problem, however, is that much of the waste land in England occurs next to people's homes, within the communities which grew up in response to the many opportunities that the industry provided. It can be derelict factory land, but it can also be an area of slum clearance waiting for redevelopment. Many children have been killed or injured by playing in abandoned buildings, by drowning in disused canals or by falling down mineshafts. They can cut themselves on broken glass. The ugly rubbish which derelict land attracts can breed vermin and flies. Perhaps what is more important, however, is that the awful atmosphere can cause complete loss of self-respect and lead to further deterioration. Waste land can drive workers and established industries away to better places, at the

Figure 1.8 Much of our wasteland occurs next to our houses; we should never have to inflict this on our children.

same time as it discourages other modern industries from coming to the area. Badly managed operational land must be included in all this.

A report in 1965 described the character of such areas as follows:

'A sense of apathy towards the living environment . . . houses not repainted, fences left to rot, kerbs broken, trees hacked about mercilessly, gardens unkempt and unused open space a mass of long grass, weeds and rubbish'.

No-one should have to grow up and live in such an environment. Children, surely, should be of great concern. We should not expect them to have to put up with dereliction around their homes for more than half their childhood, which means about six years. Yet many areas have been left far longer than this and have experienced a rapid downward trend with the onset of dereliction. Derelict and neglected land is a waste and an insult, a waste of our most scarce and valuable resource, the land, and an insult to humanity.

Chapter 2　　　　　　　　**The Continuing Problem**

2.1 New waste land

The vast legacy of waste land in Britain is increasing, despite greater efforts of restoration of the land to its former health, or reclamation to some new use. It is obvious that new areas of waste land are continually emerging. The DoE surveys of derelict land show that the areas of 'traditional' dereliction (spoil heaps, pits and military and railway land), justifying restoration or reclamation, have all fallen since 1974, and it is only the large increase in 'other forms of dereliction' (mostly urban dereliction such as former industrial sites and redundant gas works, docks and power stations) which has boosted the overall total. It is therefore important to identify the reasons why dereliction and neglect continue to appear. In this respect the causes of derelict and neglected land in inner cities, so near to people, are of particular concern.

2.2 Urban and industrial land

The vast majority of waste land in urban areas is caused mainly by sites which become vacant from various reasons and remain undeveloped. Unfortunately, this is not just a thing of the past. Land becomes vacant after housing clearance work if no new houses are built, or when an industry ceases and no new industry appears instead. Land may become vacant when there are redevelopment plans but these are delayed in a period of economic decline. Land may also be located in a depressed region now unsuitable for houses or industry. Land belonging to pubic bodies such as the gas authorities or British Rail may become disused due to a reduction of operations.

In urban areas, private owners and local authorities are often reluctant to carry out reclamation as the vacant land retains a high book value. In its vacant state, the land is then extremely hard to sell and developers obviously prefer cheaper, less difficult green field sites. At the same time, local authorities often cannot afford to maintain liabilities of old fabric on their revenue budgets and so the land remains disused and idle.

The population explosion after the last war resulted in the establishment of new towns and large housing estates on the urban fringe. With the unforeseen decline in the population growth rate, the legislation to contain urban development by establishing green belt areas has, in the opinion of many, actually contributed to the movement of people from the town to the countryside and increased the pressure for housing on fringe farmland. It seemed in the 1950's that much of this move from the towns into the country was unavoidable and sensible. However, in fact, the unfortunate consequence has been that inner city areas are poorly used and derelict.

In the past, rapid expansion of industries and the lack of environmental controls have jointly contributed to a legacy of derelict industrial land. In recent years, concern has grown over the effects of toxic substances in the environment and there have been increasing controls over the deposit of hazardous industrial wastes. Abandoned industrial sites are often polluted by products or raw materials from their processes. Even careful handling and storage of materials cannot prevent accidental spillage which may lead to long lasting problems. There are also problems with old foundations. New industries are thus eager to seek undeveloped sites. Although no figures are available for the total area of derelict industrial

Figure 2.1   When industries decline the product is usually waste land; a disused steel works in Consett.

Figure 2.2 Even newly reclaimed open space can quickly go back to waste land.

land in England, the area is probably increasing. Certainly there is an increase in the area of industrial land not being used, exacerbated recently by decline in traditional industries.

Urban waste land is particularly a problem for the metropolitan regions, where the neglected, degraded appearance of the physical structures and open spaces seriously spoils the environmental quality not only of the inner cities, but also of outer newer housing areas. The presence of neglected and unused land encourages additional forms of environmental abuse, such as fly tipping and litter, with miserable footpaths and rubbish filled back yards. There is nothing to suggest that the amount of urban wasteland will not continue to increase unless more positive steps are taken to prevent further dereliction, although certain cities have made impressive efforts. These new inner city waste lands are obviously a priority for restoration, especially where the land could be developed for new housing. New housing in inner cities would ease the pressure on the countryside, improve the urban environment and encourage industries and other employers to move back into the urban environment.

2.3 Land used for mineral extraction

Present day planning controls, mainly the Town and Country Planning Act 1971, should be adequate to prevent dereliction arising from newly established mineral workings. It is, in general, the legacy of old sites on which there is no adequate restoration condition where there may be problems. Nevertheless, with mineral extraction processes there is a continuing need for new land from which to win minerals and on which to dispose of wastes. So we must watch the situation carefully, not only to ensure that restoration is carried out, but also to see that it is imaginative and effective, because there are many possible end points. In the 1970's approximately 5,000 hectares of land per year were taken by the mineral industries. The main minerals worked in England include coal, sand and gravel, limestone, chalk, china clay and brick clay.

Land being worked for open cast coal is restored under the provisions of the Open Cast Coal Act 1958 and the Town and Country Planning Act 1971. The smaller sites can often be worked quickly and restored. The larger sites can create substantial and longer-term disturbance, although satisfactory restoration is achieved in the end. With deep-mined coal there is the additional problem of spoil disposal. Increasing mechanisation has resulted in an increase in the proportion of waste to useable coal brought

Figure 2.3 Open cast mining for coal is of necessity a major disturbance; Whitehouse site, near Ilkeston, Derbyshire.

Figure 2.4 Sand and gravel workings are often shallow but extensive; part of about 2000 hectares near Lechlade.

to the surface. Deep mines are now producing 50-60 million tonnes of colliery spoil and existing wastes are estimated at 3000 million tonnes, covering an area of 11,000 hectares. About 200 hectares of land are taken annually for tipping. At present about 300 hectares of land are restored annually, but it seems likely that land degradation will continue since tipping is really the most common and practicable means of colliery waste disposal.

Production of sand and gravel was more than 100 million tonnes in 1973 but has since fallen to 67 million tonnes in 1982. The total area of land being taken each year by sand and gravel working is about 1,500 hectares

Figure 2.5 Magnesian limestone is an important raw material and can only be extracted from the few places where it is found; a quarry near Durham.

Figure 2.6 Disused quarries can become important refuges for plants: the very rare man orchid in a disused quarry in Essex.

and about the same amount is being restored. Sand and gravel pits need not pose severe problems of restoration, but not all pits are being reclaimed.

In contrast to sand and gravel quarries, limestone quarries rarely compete for land of high agricultural value. But they are very often situated in scenic, upland areas, and there are active limestone quarries within the boundaries of five National Parks. The method of working employs deep pits with little overburden, which generally means that only limited restoration is possible until working has ceased, and even then a satisfactory restoration is not easy. However, disused workings can become important refuges for rare plant and animal species such as the man orchid (Figure 2.6), and some have been given SSSI (Site of Special Scientific Interest) status by the Nature Conservancy Council, for instance, Millers Dale quarry in the Peak District National Park.

China clay is used as a filler or pigment in the chemical industry, as a whitener in paper and paints and in pottery etc. The working of china clay produces large quantities of waste; for 1 tonne of clay, 7-9 tonnes of waste are also produced. At present, stockpiles of china clay waste total 280 million tonnes and occupy more than 1,000 hectares of land. But there is a total of 2,807ha for which permissions have been obtained. Most of this is in the St. Austell area of Cornwall. The nature of china clay deposits poses

Figure 2.7 Brick works and clay pits are a conspicuous feature of the Bedfordshire countryside.

problems for their backfilling and restoration. Large numbers of currently inactive pits are unrestored so that working can recommence in the future in response to demands for clays of differing quality. Brick clay workings are less of a problem because they are shallow and have very little waste but, in the 1970's, the amount of new land taken per year by the industry was as much as 40 hectares.

2.4 Land used for waste disposal

Figure 2.8 Every year we are each responsible for 350kg of waste, which has to be disposed of.

We are each responsible for 350kg (770 lbs) of waste a year. Together with industrial waste, there are about 100 million tonnes to be disposed of every year. As a result, over 11,000ha of land are currently being used for waste disposal and 250ha are taken new every year. This is an immense problem of our throw-away society. Some wastes are hazardous and have to be dealt with specially – others are benign. There are, interesting new developments in recycling, for instance pulverising, sorting and composting domestic refuse to make it into a fuel and an organic fertiliser; but unfortunately there are limits to the amount of recycling like this which can be done.

Household and industrial wastes have to be disposed of onto land surfaces in special sites. But excessive use of good land is often able to be prevented, as we shall see later, by using these wastes as landfill material, to restore some of the pits and excavations left by mining. The operation has to be done with great care and whatever site is used, restoration taken through to completion. Otherwise, recently mined land, or old derelict land, restored by waste disposal, can end up, as it does on too many occasions, as the derelict or neglected land of the future.

2.5 Destruction of the countryside

Agricultural land and areas of semi-natural vegetation in England are therefore constantly under pressure from the need to win minerals. They also suffer from the need to develop housing and industrial sites. At present, the loss of agricultural land to development and other uses for the five-year period ending June 1983 is estimated to be 14,000 hectares. The destruction of our rich heritage of ancient woodlands and lowland heathlands is a cause for national concern. Between 1947 and 1980, half of the woods that had existed in England since 1600 were felled to make way for more lucrative crops of corn and fast-growing conifers. Lowland heaths have been under the plough since the early 19th century and now only a fragmented 28% of this beautiful, native habitat remain (see Figure 2.10). Against this background it is clear that we must do whatever we can to protect the countryside from further destruction. Amongst all the many pressures on our countryside, as well as on our towns, it is imperative that the continuing emergence of waste land must be halted.

Figure 2.9 The continuing production of waste land must not threaten our heritage of unspoilt countryside; an ancient oak woodland is irreplaceable.

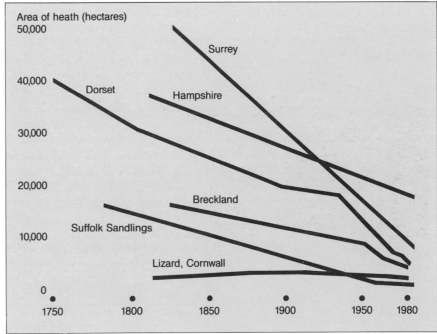

Figure 2.10 The disappearance of heathland in lowland Britain provides a strong argument for protection of wild and semi-natural areas.

21

Chapter 3   Land Can Be Recycled

3.1 Pessimism replaced by common sense

Against such a gloomy background the future looks bleak. Yet it need not be. Although the amount of derelict land increased from 1974 to 1982, at the same time over 16,000 hectares were reclaimed, an area equal to that occupied by the town of Rochester in Kent. Over the same period over 26,000 hectares of mineral workings were restored. The idea that land cannot be re-used and restored is a fallacy. If we choose to, we can treat land like any other recyclable resource (Figure 3.1). We do not have to wait and wonder about doing something, either we can complete the cycle or exploit all the ways in which derelict and neglected land can be put to new use. The figures for a single county, Cheshire (Table 3.1) show how much this is already occurring.

Indeed, the best time to deal with land which has had to be disturbed for the winning of mineral, or the disposal of wastes, is while the disturbance

Table 3.1   The changes in land use in Cheshire from 1974 to 1980 show the extent of land recycling that can occur within a single county.

from \ to	residential	amenity	agri.	industry	minerals	transport	wastes	education	health	totals
agriculture										2370 ha
derelict										480
vacant										600
minerals										400
wastes										170
amenity										120
residential										40
transport										20
industry										30
other										40
totals	1510 ha	870	360	400	320	290	260	210	50	4270 ha

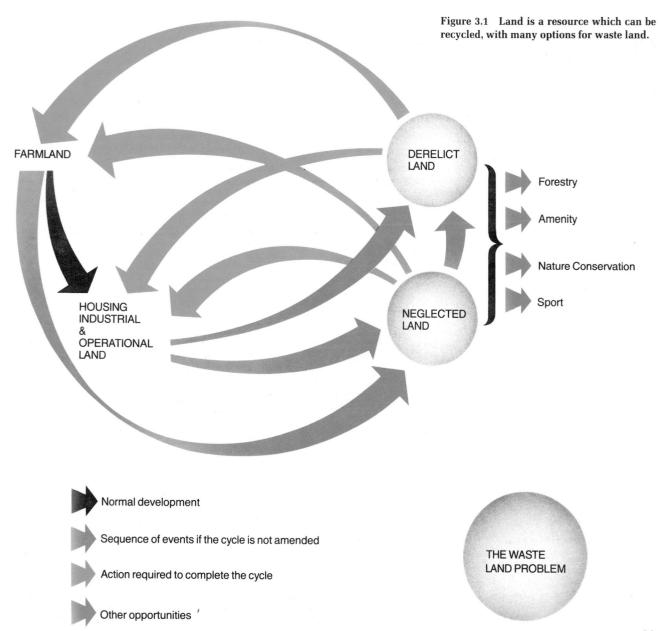

Figure 3.1 Land is a resource which can be recycled, with many options for waste land.

FARMLAND

DERELICT LAND

Forestry

Amenity

HOUSING INDUSTRIAL & OPERATIONAL LAND

Nature Conservation

Sport

NEGLECTED LAND

Normal development

Sequence of events if the cycle is not amended

Action required to complete the cycle

Other opportunities

THE WASTE LAND PROBLEM

23

is in progress and the operator and the equipment are on site. Soil and other materials can be moved economically and stored so they do not deteriorate or become misplaced. Recent government legislation will hopefully ensure that this will be the normal process. This is discussed more fully in Chapter 4.

We have, however, in England, a 45,700 hectare inheritance of derelict land, together with the much larger area of neglected and vacant land from which previous activity has disappeared. At first sight many of these areas appear to present us with an impossible task. What is less encouraging than a disused colliery spoil heap, an empty and deserted quarry or a bare pile of old mine waste in the middle of green countryside? A derelict factory site or unused slum clearance area in a town is hardly better. There are, however, two important things about these areas which mean we can look at them in quite a different light. Firstly, they have the unusual characteristic that they do not have any existing land use and so are readily available for a new use, and secondly, we now have the technology by which we can deal with their problems.

Figure 3.2 New bricks are fired with methane gas from the household refuse used to fill these obsolete brick pits; energy conservation, waste disposal and land reclamation combined.

3.2 The opportunities presented by waste land

It is obvious that before any piece of land can be used for a new purpose the old purpose has to be extinguished. Waste land has no existing use. A new development on waste land therefore not only means that some degraded land is redeemed but also that our heritage of other, good, land is not disturbed.

Most waste land is in such a poor state that it is difficult to see how any good use can be made of it. Fortunately, there is a wide variety of possibilities. Remarkable progress has been made recently in ideas for the use of waste land. What is required above all is imagination and perseverance. Some ideas are fairly straight-forward; urban wasteland can go back to housing; a gravel pit, already partially colonised by plants, can become a nature reserve. But who would think of a golf course on a chemical waste heap, or firing new bricks with the methane from household refuse used to fill the brick pits which have been finished with?

Some of the ways in which waste land can be used are given in Table 3.2. The list of possibilities is almost endless, and there are always new ideas to be tried and to be fitted into local plans and needs. In Germany, coal waste heaps are afforested and people then build week-end cottages among the trees. In the United States, an old gravel pit filled with water

Table 3.2   Some of the many uses for waste land.

Short term

waste disposal
car parking
storage
green space

Long term

production	amenity	development
arable agriculture	country parks	industry
grassland agriculture	wildife habitats	commercial development
forestry	nature reserves	housing
energy plantations	amenity woodland	public authority building
glasshouse crops	water sports	playgrounds
small scale horticulture	playing fields	roads
	camp sites	storage areas
	golf courses	reservoirs
	urban parks	
	foot paths	

Figure 3.3 A new use for a gravel pit; racing at Holme Pierpoint National Water Sport Centre.

was developed as a high class housing estate with the lake at the bottom of every garden and sold for much more than was paid for the land before the gravel was extracted. In Britain, our international rowing centre at Holme Pierpoint is an old gravel pit, and several disused railway lines have become country parks. The challenge to creative thinking in all of us, not only landscape architects and planners, is immense.

3.3 Immediate restoration

With the annual use of land for mineral extraction running at several thousand hectares a year, any delay in restoration of the land after disturbance adds to the total of waste land. This applies to any ongoing land use of this kind – such as refuse disposal or even slum clearance. There is a face-saving expression – interim land – used particularly for land cleared of old houses in cities waiting for future development. This term does not disguise the fact that the land is waste land and an assault on our well being and senses, usually in the middle of where very many people live.

The solution is to devise and build into the operation, whatever it is, a

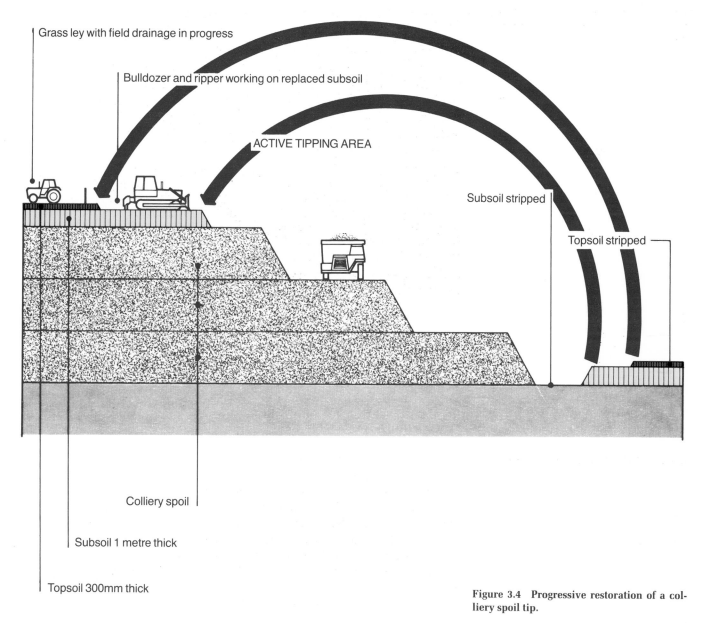

Grass ley with field drainage in progress

Bulldozer and ripper working on replaced subsoil

ACTIVE TIPPING AREA

Subsoil stripped

Topsoil stripped

Colliery spoil

Subsoil 1 metre thick

Topsoil 300mm thick

Figure 3.4 Progressive restoration of a colliery spoil tip.

system of immediate restoration, so the absolute minimum area of disturbed land is left untreated or without redevelopment. There is no physical reason at all, for instance, why clearance of obsolete houses in cities cannot be followed by rebuilding immediately. Refuse disposal sites are a very interesting case. They have to be filled and covered progressively – this is a requirement of the site licence issued in accordance with the Control of Pollution Act 1974. But the subsequent restoration to an attractive vegetation cover and appropriate land use should follow just as rapidly. Unfortunately, this often does not happen and restoration waits many years until the whole site is finished with. In the past, little attempt

Figure 3.5 Pulverised fuel ash from the power station at Drax is being deposited as a large mound on the site of a derelict ordnance depot, and immediately restored to agriculture.

was made to restore colliery spoil heaps as fast as they were formed. For the future, we can be thankful that progressive restoration was strongly recommended by the Commission on Energy and the Environment and is now being required. But there are still plenty of heaps where it has not yet started.

One outstanding example of immediate, progressive restoration is the site at Barlow where 1800 tonnes of pulverised fuel ash from Drax power station are disposed of every day onto a derelict site left by a munitions dump; at any one time only seven hectares are bare and new agricultural land is restored within six months of the ash being tipped. Another is the quarry of the cement works at Dumbarton; restoration is a continuous part of the extraction process. As far as possible the same applies on open-cast coal sites, although there must always be some land, apart from the extraction area itself, set aside for temporary storage heaps etc.

These examples (and there are many others) however, are not successful by accident. They are the result of some very positive thinking before the operations even began. There has to be some careful planning if new housing developments are to follow quickly on the old. This should hardly be difficult. If a green site is to be restored, top soils and subsoils must be carefully preserved and replaced as fast as possible without being muddled or compacted. Perfect success in this sort of work can be at the mercy of the weather and operational problems, but with improved techniques and machinery the whole process is considerably easier than it was.

Normally the original soils and land use are reinstated as they were; many people think that this is always the best procedure. Often it is, but in the course of the disturbance it may be possible to bring up to the surface soil-forming materials which are better than those that were originally present, and therby improve the quality of the land. Some subsoils can actually be of better quality than top soils. Difficult materials can be buried. In a number of cases where opencast mining for coal is taking place, old colliery spoil heaps or workings from a previous underground mine can be removed and buried. But all this requires careful site surveys and planning before the operation begins (see Table 5.1).

In some cases it is impossible to reinstate the original land use, for instance, in a low-lying gravel pit in agricultural land which fills up with water after excavation. For these, a new land use has to be devised, such as water sports or nature conservation, which not only provides for a real

Figure 3.6   Inspecting the new pasture laid down on the fuel ash waste heap at Drax; the restoration is immediate.

need, but may also pay for the subsequent management, or even produce a revenue. Again, there is no reason why restoration to the new land use should not proceed immediately, providing operational requirements do not prevent it.

3.4 Management within ongoing operations

Operational land, the land which is needed for actual workings or other developments, should be kept as small as possible by ensuring that the final restoration follows with the minimum of delay. But there is much more that can be done to reduce its impact.

Firstly, any waste or overburden material itself can be placed immediately in such a way that it hides the operation. This will also reduce the spread of noise from the operation. Many planning authorities already insist on this before they give permission. If this waste is to be permanent, then its outside edges at least can be landscaped immediately so that the new landscape has a chance to develop early. If the material is only a temporary screen, it can still be covered temporarily with vegetation at

Figure 3.7 This gorse and lupin covered slope is the newly-restored first lift of what will ultimately be a large china clay waste heap; Lee Moor near Plymouth.

very little expense. Grasses and legumes, such as red and white clover and lucerne, grow and cover quickly, preventing erosion.

Where a waste heap is to be large and permanent the first lift or tier can be vegetated with the final cover while the second and third lifts are still being deposited. It should be normal practice in this country that a vegetation cover is established on the outside faces of all waste heaps as soon as they are finished. Unfortunately, this is not always the case.

There are many situations where screening by waste heaps is not possible. In this case, trees and shrubs can be planted on the surrounding land. But, firstly, the trees are often not planted early enough or looked after well enough to form a good screen, and secondly, they are often planted in such regimented rows that they actually draw attention to the workings rather than hide them.

3.5 Dealing with dereliction from the past

Figure 3.8 New uses for an old landscape; Central Forest Park, in Hanley, Stoke-on-Trent, has been created from old coal workings.

In many derelict sites the original soil has been lost or badly spoilt. Sometimes there may even be toxic materials on the site. In these cases, money will have to be spent to rectify the problems and restore a satisfactory soil, or land surface suitable for building if required, before the new development can take place. Expensive treatment may seem an insuperable obstacle. But a whole range of techniques are now available (see Chapter 5), some of which are very simple and inexpensive, yet effective. Also, the Government's system of grants for derelict land reclamation are available to local authorities and to private land owners. In addition, there are other sources of financial support (see Chapter 4).

The opportunities that derelict sites offer means that net expenditure may be nil. There is now, for instance, a serious problem of finding sites for waste disposal – especially domestic and non-hazardous industrial wastes. A derelict site may be ideally suitable, particularly if it is an old quarry or similar excavation.

The waste can be used for restoring the original land levels – remembering to allow substantial amounts for shrinkage as the waste decays and compacts. The surface of the waste can then be restored, and the whole operation carried out at a net profit, because of the amount that can be charged for receiving the refuse for disposal in the first place. There can be problems from gas and leachate emissions from the waste, but these can be obviated and the gas even used for heating and other purposes. Other materials such as pulverised fuel ash from power stations are easier to use; at the moment the old brick pits near Peterborough are being filled with ash from the Trent Valley power stations at the rate of 600,000 tonnes per year.

Derelict land in or near cities can be put to immediate, profitable, other new uses, such as factories or housing, after basic reclamation work has been carried out, so that the whole operation pays for itself and the city is restored. It would be absurd if we did not pursue such land end uses wherever they are possible. Otherwise we may end up with towns turning into half-baked country, while the nearby countryside is being turned into town.

There have been a number of occasions where an area of waste land has consisted of a part which was completely derelict, and part merely neglected and of low value because of the adjacent unappealing derelict land. In such cases, expenditure by a local authority on purchase of the whole area and simple restoration of the derelict land portion, so improved the value of the neglected area and its attractiveness for developers for housing and industry, that the cost of the whole scheme was met by the final resale of the once neglected land so that, again, there is no cost to the taxpayer.

Some sites, such as subsidence flashes, almost beg to be passed on to a new use such as water sports, and are only waiting for original owners and planners to make up their minds to finish with the past and get on with the new.

In many situations, however, particularly in the north of England where there has been such a major decline in industrial activity, it may not be so easy to find a major financial return for the land after restoration. The distribution of derelict land shown in Figure 1.7 makes this clear. In these situations, if appropriate grant aid is not available, it may be necessary to look for simple low cost treatments so that these areas do not inflict their ugliness and environmental problems on the people who surround them. Low cost techniques are much more readily available than many realise. Urban derelict areas, for instance, which are not going to be used for housing or industry can be reclaimed very inexpensively to informal recreation by simple seeding and fertilising directly on to the brick rubble itself (see Chapter 5). The technique is sufficiently cheap to be used on land which is only temporarily derelict and is due for proper redevelopment within a few years. In this respect neglected land may be extremely easy to treat. With a simple tidying up and perhaps ploughing and

Figure 3.9 Temporarily cleared urban areas can be quickly improved by sowing grass directly onto the brick rubble; Grove St., Liverpool after one year.

reseeding, an area can be brought back to low intensity but profitable agriculture. Perhaps the simplest treatment is silage or other forms of grass cropping, which may well be able to be carried out by a nearby farming contractor.

In the past, on loose tipped waste heaps from coal mines and ironstone workings in particular, forest trees have been planted, using small transplants. This was done because it was one of the cheapest ways in which derelict land could be dealt with. The people who did it were pioneers of land reclamation and did not expect anything more than to hide the eyesores which had become their responsibilities. A recent survey of these old sites by the Forestry Commission has shown that so long as the wastes were loose tipped, not consolidated, and without special problems, such as acidity, the growth of the trees has proved to be as good as on normal sites. Many of these sites, for instance in Durham, Lancashire and Northamptonshire, are now very beautiful additions to the landscape (see Figure 7.6). They also have commercial potential.

A new low cost technique which is being developed is direct seeding of trees and shrubs, choosing species which are native and adapted to the site

Figure 3.10 Rock faces in quarries can be quickly and easily revegetated; this rock face at Tunstead in the Peak District was treated with a mixture of sewage sludge and wild plant seed.

Figure 3.11   The disused limestone quarry at Millers Dale in Derbyshire has become an important site for wildlife.

in question, without any expensive earthmoving beforehand. This can be carried out even on very rough and irregular surfaces, such as a rock face. A variation is to mix the seeds with sewage sludge or some equivalent slurry, and pour or spray the mixture on the surface to be treated. Such techniques are unlikely ever to give a commercial return but will provide an attractive natural vegetation cover.

Of course, the very simplest and cheapest method of revegetation is to allow nature to do the work for us. The trouble is that in many situations nature takes time – seedlings have to become established and soil fertility has to accumulate. But there are a large number of derelict sites which have been left for long enough to have become colonised, often with interesting and beautiful plants, such as orchids. In others, the missing species can be introduced and left to prosper without any further help. The low fertility of the sites prevents vigorous species from swamping the soil surface, and allows species sensitive to competition to find a refuge. The results are sometimes quite stunning (Fig. 3.11).

As a result, many derelict areas have been adopted by local conservation groups and local authorities as nature reserves and general amenity areas at little or no cost to the taxpayer, to be enjoyed by everyone. In a land where farming is steadily becoming more intensive and wilderness is disappearing, derelict areas have an important role to play both for amenity and to protect endangered and unusual species. Such areas may require tidying up and fencing to stop illegal tipping but little more.

There remains a hard core of land for which the only answer seems to be rather expensive treatment if it is not to remain a threat to our well-being, not only in terms of visual offence, but also in terms of pollution and other serious environmental problems. Obvious examples are large colliery spoil and metalliferous mine waste heaps, and certain types of old industrial sites. These are the sort of areas for which government grants are essential. They are a legacy of less caring attitudes for the environment and economic change. Their restoration depends on the sophisticated techniques which have been developed over the last two decades, which are discussed in Chapter 5. They may be just the sites where new industry can and should be established in the future.

But even for these there may be ways of paying for the restoration, as the result of the development of new mining extraction techniques. Old colliery spoils can contain considerable quantities of good coal, which can now, with modern techniques, be extracted at a profit, sufficient to pay for the subsequent restoration of the reprocessed spoil. Metal mine wastes produced by inefficient processes of the past may contain enough metal to be profitably reprocessed by new mobile plants specially designed for small quantities. In this case, sufficient metal may be removed that the waste becomes no longer toxic and so can be restored more cheaply.

Where such economies cannot be found, the site will have to be tackled head on. It must be looked at carefully and with imagination, to work out the best end point and the minimum work needed to get the maximum result. In the days when the great British landscape tradition was being established, Alexander Pope required us to look for the 'genius of the place' and Capability Brown offered to bring out for his clients 'the capability' of their estates. We have to do the same today, whether it is for factory or for green field, and at the same time employ the techniques to ensure that ideas of the imagination are successfully realised in practice.

Figure 3.12 New techniques enable some discarded wastes to be reprocessed at a profit, sufficient to pay for their subsequent reclamation; a coal washery on colliery spoil in Lancashire.

Chapter 4

Government Policies for Reducing Waste Land

4.1 The general approach

Figure 4.1 New mining operations can re-move old dereliction; the old mine workings at Ramcroft (top picture) were tidied away by a recent opencast operation which restored the land to agriculture (bottom).

If the situation is to improve and not get worse, it has to be the responsibility of successive governments to develop and maintain a workable and effective policy. This must firstly, lead to a reduction of the existing wasteland, and secondly prevent, as far as is possible, any further wasteland forming. Such a policy needs to be directed in particular towards the worse type of waste land – the officially derelict land. Perfect solutions are not likely to be easy; there must be prevention as well as cure.

The crucial curative legislation, designed to reduce the total of existing wasteland, is the Derelict Land Act 1982 which was preceded by a number of Acts including the Local Government Act, 1966. This makes grants available for the reclamation of land which is derelict, neglected or unsightly. Under the Act, local authorities have powers, but no statutory duty, to acquire and reclaim derelict land. In England, Central Government grants are available both to local authorities and to the non-local authority sector for the reclamation of derelict land for the purpose of bringing it into use or improving its appearance. However, much of the problem of our urban environment is caused by land which is not 'derelict' but vacant or under used. Unfortunately, there is no direct fiscal mechanism for dealing with this; it is a product of the present depressed state of our economy.

The main preventative legislation, which is designed to limit the production of further wasteland, is the Town and Country Planning Act 1971 which for mineral working has been amended by the Town and Country Planning (Minerals) Act of 1981. This defines mineral planning authorities and gives them powers to control the environmental effects of mineral working. Authorities have been given the power to require the tidying up of sites where mineral working has been suspended, and where it has ceased authorities may prohibit the resumption of working without a fresh grant of planning permission and may impose tidying-up and restoration requirements. Where there is a restoration condition, the Act empowers authorities to impose aftercare conditions, requiring steps to be taken to plant, cultivate, fertilise, water, drain or otherwise treat restored land so as to bring it to the standard required for agriculture, forestry or amenity use (DoE circular 1/82).

4.2 Grant aid to promote land restoration

Various policies and programmes have been made available to encourage the recycling of land, particularly in urban areas. What is important is the way these Acts and other policies work in practice. Because of industrial and social changes, even the most careful legislation will never be able to prevent new derelict land occurring and any policy has to cope with developments in the future as well as what has already taken place.

(a) *Derelict Land Grants*
In officially recognised Assisted Areas and Derelict Land Clearance Areas, substantial grants are available for derelict land reclamation, at the rate of 100% of the net loss for local authorities and English Estates and 80% for all other land owners. Outside these areas the rate is 50% for both local authorities and others, except that in the National Parks and Areas of Outstanding Natural Beauty local authorities can receive 75% grants. 50% grants to local authorities are normally payable for 60 years on the notional annual loan charges. Grants at the 100% and 75% rates and grants to the non-local authority sector are paid as a lump sum.

Although grants under this system are given only for sites falling under the definition of 'derelict', provision is made to include additional land which is not derelict but is required to aid the reclamation works. Of the 17,000 hectares of derelict land restored between 1974 and 1982, about 60% of it was with the aid of derelict land grants. In 1984/5 the expenditure provision for the local authority was £69m (1978/9 £21·2m) and the grant aid available for non-local authority schemes was £5m (1981/2, £0·6m). For the former, priority is being given to joint schemes by local authorities and private developers (Category A schemes) aimed at bringing land reclaimed by public expenditure into private development for industrial, commercial, housing, recreational or other uses. These will account for 35% of the programme in 1984/5. Resources are also earmarked annually for special schemes, e.g. reclamation of former steel works, land for garden festivals, for coal tip reclamation, and miscellaneous derelict land on the urban fringe under the Groundwork Trust

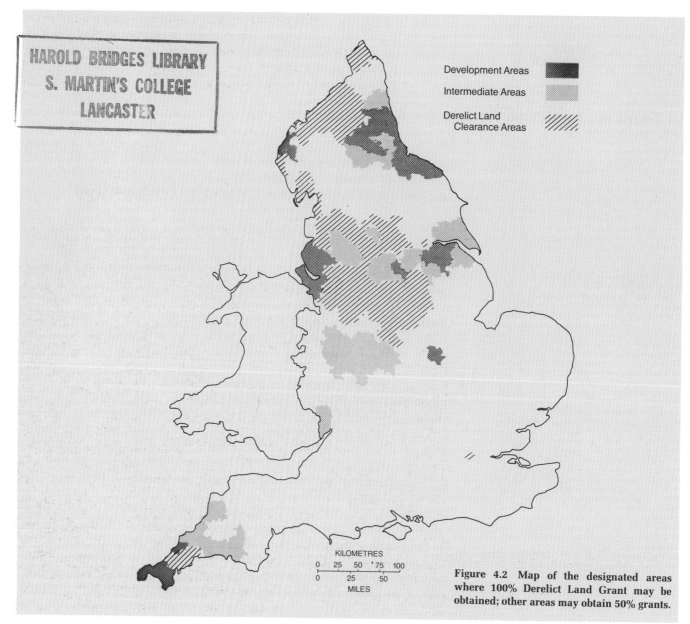

Development Areas

Intermediate Areas

Derelict Land
Clearance Areas

KILOMETRES

0   25   50   75   100

0   25   50

MILES

Figure 4.2 Map of the designated areas where 100% Derelict Land Grant may be obtained; other areas may obtain 50% grants.

programme. In 1978/9 open space, agriculture and forestry accounted for the bulk of the land involved in schemes approved for grant and only 6% was for 'hard' development uses. In recent years, much greater emphasis has been placed on reclamation for development and in 1983/84 'hard' development end uses, mainly industrial and residential, accounted for 60% of the land in approved schemes.

Grants can be paid to local authorities towards expenditure on the following items:

(i) land acquisition

(ii) site surveys and investigations

(iii) reclamation works, i.e. all costs necessary to bring the land to the equivalent of a green field site

(iv) follow-up treatment to ensure successful establishment of grass and/ or trees

Figure 4.3 A special grant has been given to Stoke-on-Trent for the reclamation of Shelton Bar Steelworks for a National Garden Festival.

(v) basic infrastructure on or off site, depending on the scheme, e.g. water, sewerage, access roads etc. but restricted to provision of common services

(vi) administrative expenses on a sliding scale up to a maximum of 15% of the works costs (since April 1985)

(vii) consultants fees

(viii) removal of derelict or obsolete industrial buildings

(ix) works necessary to release sites which are land-locked and which need work done to open up their potential development value

Some costs are clearly not eligible for grant, e.g. for clearing natural dereliction, for reclaiming land which is in active use or disused mineral workings or spoil heaps which are covered by enforceable restoration conditions.

Grants only cover the net loss incurred by the local authority carrying out the reclamation scheme. Normally, the grants are paid initially on the gross expenditure incurred. Then when the land is disposed of, the value of the land after reclamation is set off against the approved total expenditure to determine the amount of the grant to be recovered (see Table 4.1). This 'betterment value' can be a severe stumbling block. Reclaimed land retained by a local authority for amenity or open space is treated as having a nil after-value.

Grants to other landowners, including nationalised industries, were first introduced in the Local Government Planning and Land Act 1980. In Assisted Areas and Derelict Land Clearance Areas they are payable on 80% of the net loss incurred by the landowner in carrying out the reclamation works only, allowing for changes in land value. Elsewhere the rate of grant is 50%. They do not pay for land acquisition, infrastructure, administrative expenses, or for schemes on neglected land. The grants are paid on satisfactory completion of approved schemes. They are becoming an important way of enabling derelict land to be reclaimed without local authority involvement and without its ownership having to be acquired by them.

Application for a Derelict Land Grant can be made by anyone, on a form which is obtainable from regional offices of the Department of the Environment.

Table 4.1 Formula for recovery of Derelict Land Grant

A. Where Local Authority does not own land and grant is paid for acquisition

Let a = actual cost of land acquisition

　　b = cost of reclamation

　　c = proceeds of sale of land on disposal

Grant paid initially (if at 100%) will equal a + b.

Subject to amount recovered not exceeding a + b and assuming that c − a is positive, the amount recovered shall be $a + \dfrac{c - a}{2}$

B. Where Local Authority already owns land

Let a = estimated current value of land before reclamation

　　b = cost of reclamation

　　c = proceeds of sale of land on disposal

Grant paid initially (if at 100%) will equal b.

Subject to the amount recovered not exceeding b and assuming that c − a is positive, the amount recovered shall be $\dfrac{c - a}{2}$

C. Where grant rate is 50%

The amount recovered shall be half that calculated in accordance with the appropriate formula above.

(b) *Small Clearance Schemes on Non-Derelict Land*

Since 1982 grant has been available for less expensive clearance schemes for land which is not derelict within the administrative definition but merely neglected or unsightly. For grant purposes, neglected or unsightly land is land which, although capable of beneficial use, is at present uncared for, untidy, and in a condition detrimental to the environment. This includes small vacant sites, possibly awaiting development but without immediate prospect of it, small or odd-shaped areas of land unsuitable for development, which have been neglected, and minor dilapidated structures.

Neglected or unsightly sites can only be tackled by local authorities on their own land or, by agreement, on land owned by other persons. However, Section 65 of the Town and Country Planning Act 1971 enables a local authority to require an owner of land to abate any serious injury caused to the amenity of the area by the condition of their land. Thus grant is given in respect of privately owned land only where action under Section 65 is not practicable.

Application for a grant in respect of a small clearance scheme must be made through the Regional Offices of the Department of the Environment. The scheme must cost no more than £10,000.

(c) *Urban Programme Grants*

Wide ranging support has been made available under the Inner Urban Areas Act 1978 to provide special funds for those inner cities with the greatest amount or urban deprivation, particularly in relation to unemployment. These funds are available to Local Authorities only, but can be used for a wide variety of purposes including the treatment of neglected areas which would not be covered by Derelict Land Grant. The funds can be used to take land being reclaimed with a Derelict Land Grant to the next stage of development.

To obtain support Local Authorities have only, in the first instance, to get broad endorsement for a programme not worked out in site by site

Figure 4.4 A very small area of urban clearance land turned over to an inner city playgroup and reclaimed with an Urban Programme Grant and the help of a local community agency.

detail. The grants cover only 75% of the cost; the rest has to be provided by the Local Authorities themselves. For this reason the scheme was introduced as the Inner City Partnership Programme.

Because of the freedom over use and the wide variety of problems which can be tackled, the support has been widely used. Peripheral problems which are often the underlying cause of wasteland development can be dealt with. In 1984/85 proposed expenditure was £224m in the partnership and programme authorities; £44m on environmental projects, £85m on economic and £95m on social.

(d) *Urban Development Grants*

To encourage joint local authority/private sector participation in urban development projects designed to attract more private development into inner city areas, Urban Development Grants were introduced in 1982. All local authorities designated under the Inner Urban Areas Act 1978 and those with an Enterprise Zone are invited to submit applications for support for work intended to create opportunities for the private sector to carry out projects which would not otherwise go ahead. Grants are normally 75% of the local authorities' costs and are not payable direct to private developers.

Many Urban Development Grant schemes involve vacant or derelict land or buildings. 89 such schemes have so far received offers of grant. £44m grant expenditure is evoking a total potential private sector investment of £215m. The total area of the sites is 184 hectares and the schemes include industrial, commercial, housing and hotel development and also recreational and leisure facilities.

Some projects may be eligible for a package of grants, e.g. Derelict Land Grant, Urban Development Grant and Regional Development Grant (payable by Department of Industry towards capital cost of providing new buildings, works, plant and machinery in Special Development and Development Areas). The first call on resources is normally the Derelict Land Grant and the amount paid is taken into account in determining the appropriate level of Urban Development Grant.

(e) *Urban Development Corporations*

Urban Development Corporations, similar to New Town Corporations, have been established in London and Merseyside to regenerate substantial areas of predominantly derelict land, much of it former docks or land previously owned by public sector bodies. The corporations are particularly concerned to prepare difficult sites for disposal to the private sector. This is unlikely to be profitable and so they are financed by 100% Government grants and by recycling receipts from land disposals. Their expenditure involves the acquisition, reclamation and servicing of land and buildings for resale for housing, commerce and industry, the provision of infrastructure and environmental improvements and the provision of better social facilities.

A substantial part of Merseyside Development Corporation's efforts, for instance, were initially directed to the International Garden Festival which opened in May 1984. This involved the reclamation of 250 acres of derelict land to be sold subsequently. Disused docks and dock buildings are also being restored at a total cost of £10·6m in 1983/4 for sale as soon as developers can be found.

(f) *Groundwork Trusts*
In addition to the schemes aimed at bringing development back into urban and industrial areas, other schemes of environmental improvement have also received financial assistance. Six Groundwork Trusts have been set

Figure 4.5 Groundwork Trusts have been set up to improve the environment in run-down urban fringe areas; hard work on a small area of neglected land at Sutton Manor near St. Helens.

up by the Countryside Commission to help establish environmental improvement schemes in rundown urban fringes. The Groundwork movement aims to bring together public, private and voluntary interests in a co-ordinated effort to upgrade the environment, to realise the full potential of under-used land, to convert waste land to productive uses, and to improve access to the countryside for recreation and enjoyment.

Resources for Groundwork Trusts are made available by the Countryside Commission and local authorities. Each Trust is operating on a revenue budget of approximately £100,000 per annum and has been given the difficult task of becoming increasingly financially self-sufficient. At the same time special allocations of Derelict Land Grant have been made to the local authorities, but not the Trusts involved, in each Groundwork area.

(g) *Manpower Services Commission Special Programmes*
Environmental schemes may be carried out by school, college or university leavers via the Community Projects (CP) Scheme, under the Youth Training Scheme (YTS) and the Community Enterprise Programme (CEP). The primary aim of these is to provide work experience for the unemployed on projects of community benefit. In general, only manpower costs can be funded, including where appropriate, skilled supervision, with a small allowance for materials and design of projects.

(h) *Countryside Commission and Sports Council Grants*
Grants for tree planting are available from the Countryside Commission. Grant aid for amenity planting only is considered. Grants may also be available from the Sports Council and the Countryside Commission towards the cost incurred in the development of sites for sport and recreation.

(i) *Forestry Grant Scheme*
The Forestry Commission has provided grant aid towards the cost of tree planting by private owners. There have been various schemes over the years but the only one now open to new applicants is the Forestry Grant Scheme. The scheme caters for individual areas of 0.25 hectares and over and is open to both owners and tenants. Commercial timber production must usually be the primary objective. The rate of grant varies according to the total area of the wood and there are higher rates for broadleaves than

for conifers. Grants are also payable for the rehabilitation of existing woodlands. Further details are given in a free booklet 'Forestry Grant Scheme', available from the Forestry Commission.

4.3 Planning policies to promote land restoration and good land use

No society can exist without laws to ensure good behaviour. This is as true for land use as for anything else. There have to be regulations determining how land is treated, requiring work to be carried out in ways which, from a strictly personal or commercial point of view, might not be advantageous but which are important for the community and for future generations. Such planning regulations may sometimes be criticised, but they are essential, and are an integral part of control over wasteland.

(a) *Mineral workings*
There are no statutory requirements for local authorities or private land owners to carry out land restoration in urban areas – something we should perhaps ponder over. However, for land which has been affected by mineral working, new planning controls have been introduced in the Town and Country Planning (Minerals) Act 1981. Since 1947, all mineral operators, except the National Coal Board, have had to seek planning

Figure 4.6 The operators of mineral workings realise that they may be refused further planning permissions if their track record is not good; a well restored sand and gravel working at Hatfield, Hertfordshire.

permission for the continuance of existing workings as well as for the opening of new ones. Mineral operators are required to restore sites to a suitable after-use in accordance with the 'polluter pays' principle. The restoration is not grant-aided. The incentive to achieve high standards of restoration is the possibility of refusal of future applications by the planning authorities, who may take into account the relevant track record of the mineral operator. These standards are set in relation to the local situation, taking into consideration the benefits that can be achieved and the costs they impose on the industry. By 1982 there were over 100,000ha of land covered by planning permission for surface mineral workings.

The form of restoration required will depend very much on the type of deposit, the nature of the excavation and the availability of fill material. In the case of larger sites, progressive restoration may be required, particularly where working can be phased. The restoration of a mineral working to original ground level will depend on the availability of filling materials, whether generated on-site or imported from elsewhere. There is no single solution required – it is very much 'best practicable means'.

It is obviously essential for the mineral operator to discuss with the mineral planning authority at an early stage the type of restoration and after-care desirable, and the steps for achieving it. Consultation with the

Figure 4.7   When land is restored to forestry, consultation with the Forestry Commission is essential; 10 years growth of pine trees after sand and gravel extraction at Bramshill Warren, Hampshire.

appropriate Minister (in practice ADAS), or the Forestry Commission are required before schemes for agriculture or forestry are approved.

All applications are made to the district planning authority who refer mineral applications to the county planning authority. Applications have to be made on a form obtained from the local planning authority.

(b) *Waste Disposal Management*
The great bulk of waste is disposed of in holes in the ground or on other, often derelict, sites. The objective is firstly to dispose of waste in an environmentally secure manner, but secondly, in most cases to restore land for some positive purpose though seldom for substantial building, even in the longer term (say 30 years).

The Control of Pollution Act 1974 is the principal Act regulating and controlling the disposal of waste. It affects a waste disposal operation in three main ways. Firstly, it requires that the waste disposal authority prepares a waste disposal plan for its area. Secondly, it requires that a landfill site is licensed before operations can commence. This licence, which can be revoked or modified, sets the conditions within which the landfill operation will be conducted. Thirdly, the Act makes provision for the control of discharges.

Wastes are carefully classified and each site is licensed to receive only particular wastes. Hazardous wastes are now deposited at only a very few sites within the country. To take care of this, local authorities in England spent £197m (net revenue) and £46m (capital) on waste disposal in 1982/3. About 80% of waste disposal positively contributes to the restoration of holes in the ground or other dereliction.

(c) *Contaminated land and pollution control*
Land formerly used for industry or waste disposal may have become contaminated with toxic substances which can impose constraints on subsequent reclamation and re-use. To prevent further contamination of land in the future, the Control of Pollution Act 1974 was introduced to give provisions for dealing with waste on land, pollution of water, noise, pollution of the atmosphere and miscellaneous other issues. Responsibility for pollution control rests in general with local and water authorities who can bring pressure to bear on individuals and companies causing pollution, if necessary by requiring the complete closure of the operation concerned. This is obviously a very powerful tool, which rarely has to be

applied. More commonly, where necessary, a 'stop' notice is served requiring that the particular operation is stopped until the problem has been remedied.

(d) *Proper maintenance of waste land*

All the legislation appears to be weighted toward control of mineral and waste disposal operations. Yet in the Town and Country Planning Act 1971 there is a section 65 where local authorities are given the power, if it appears that the amenity of any part of their area is being seriously injured by the condition of a garden or vacant site, to require the owner and occupier to maintain or restore the land properly. This is a remarkable piece of legislation which could be immensely valuable in improving the condition of wasteland, especially in cities. However, it is rarely used and one of the reasons may be that local authorities have found difficulties in interpretation, such as, what constitutes, 'open land' or, 'serious injury to amenity' The Government are considering clarifying the provisions to make them easier to use.

(e) *Land Registers*

We have said very little about neglected land, usually in a poor state only because nobody is doing anything about it. It is a problem very difficult to legislate for. But under Part X of the Local Government, Planning and Land Act 1980, vacant or underused land in public ownership, of an acre (0.4ha) or more in extent, has been recorded in land registers maintained by the DoE. At 1st January 1985 there were 11,500 sites (44860ha) on the registers. By this, the existence of neglected land is made far more widely known. About 45% of all these sites have been judged to have medium or high potential for development, the others little or none. As a result by early 1985, 6540ha had been removed from the registers following sale and 2840ha because the land had been brought into use.

(f) *Nature Conservation and Planning*

The final part of the planning armoury which can limit wasteland concerns nature conservation. The increasing pressures on land, for example, from development and recreation, often compete and conflict with the aim of conserving the remaining relatively natural elements of the environment in Britain. As a result many sites of particular nature conservation importance have been given statutory designations of

National Nature Reserve (NNR), Local Nature Reserve (LNR), or Site of Special Scientific Interest (SSSI). By this, these sites and reserves can be protected from damage or destruction and their important scientific features conserved. The Town and Country Planning GDO 1977 ensures that the Nature Conservancy Council is consulted by planning authorities 14 days before permission can be granted for the development of land in an SSSI. However, there is at present a 3 month interval between the notification of an SSSI by the NCC and its instatement, during which time the site can be damaged. Local authorities may protect and regulate their own LNRs by making byelaws under the National Parks and Access to the Countryside Act 1949. NNRs are of national or international importance and local planning authorities are obliged to treat NNRs as Crown Land under the Town and Country Planning Act 1971 (See DoE circular 108/77).

Chapter 5

Methods of Restoring Waste Land

5.1 What is practicable?

Figure 5.1 Urban derelict land can be treated and developed for housing.

The magnitude of the problem is clear, the opportunities that waste land presents are considerable, and financial support is available. The questions that remain concern the difficulty of restoration and its cost. Any enthusiasm for land restoration will soon disappear if the whole operation is too complex and too costly.

It must be remembered that, although there is still a large amount of waste land, in the last decade over 16,000 hectares of derelict land have been restored, and, at the same time, over 26,000 hectares of mineral workings have been reinstated. Anyone visiting most of that land now would not imagine that it has ever been derelict or worked for minerals, unless they had seen it previously. Successful restoration certainly is possible and is easily implemented. But proper techniques must be used; in 1982, there were 5000 hectares of land for which the reclamation was officially judged as unsatisfactory.

5.2 Initial steps

No matter what the intended use is, the pre-requisite for all reclamation is a proper appraisal of both the shape and the detailed nature of the site. Only by this can the problems and potential of the site be properly understood and sensible decisions made about the final land use. Land use must be related to the site conditions as well as to local planning requirements. There is no sense, for instance, planning to establish housing on an urban site if the previous land use has left high levels of toxicity in the ground, or burying a large amount of material considered to be waste when it would make a first class final covering of the site.

Any survey must cover a number of important points, shown in Table 5.1. None of these is particularly expensive or difficult to carry out and there are consultants and laboratories who specialise in this sort of work (see Appendix II).

Following this, the proposed land use can be confirmed, adjusted or changed, ownership and finance sorted out and a detailed programme for the restoration and redevelopment of the area prepared. Each end point

Table 5.1 How to appraise waste land – the major steps

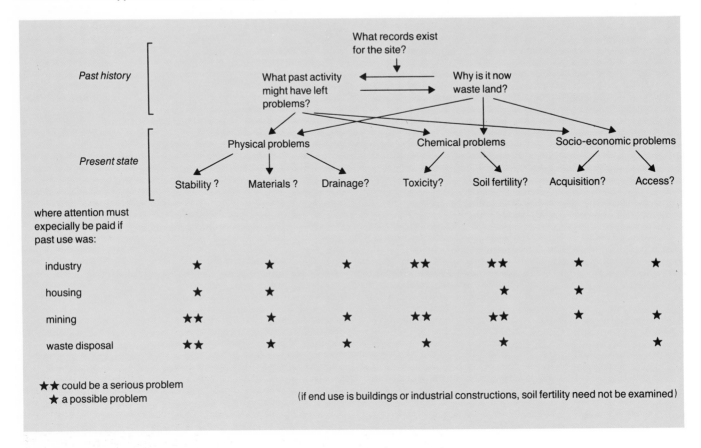

has its own particular requirements and restoration techniques by which the land can most effectively be returned to use. So a properly planned programme is essential.

5.3 Building houses and factories

In the past, there has been a great tendency for developers to avoid waste land because of the possibility of contamination, ground instability and the presence of old foundations and other structures. This has led them to choose green field sites instead. The treatment of contamination is discussed in section 5.7. It must be remembered that many types of ground contamination are best contained by the hard surfaces needed for industrial development and that to put a new industry where there has previously been industry, is both feasible and sensible.

The problem of ground instability is more difficult. Loose tipped wastes which have never been consolidated are obviously the worst problem. If the waste is not too deep, local removal and replacement by a more suitable material can be carried out, as in the foundations of the pavillion for the Liverpool International Garden Festival. Alternatively, piled foundations through to the solid ground beneath can be constructed as at Gateshead (Case Study 6.16). But for light and small structures the material can be locally densified. One way is to pre-load the waste temporarily with a surcharge of waste or indeed any heavy material. The loose waste is compressed immediately and so the surcharge can be moved progressively around the site. Another method is to drop a very heavy weight from a substantial height (about 150 tonnes from 20 metres). There are also various new vibration treatments which shake the material into a denser more compact state. These techniques are not excessively expensive. But if they cannot be used, these types of sites will have to go to other uses.

The stability of tipped materials which were consolidated during tipping should be satisfactory for building purposes. However, it is sometimes difficult to be certain that consolidation has not left local soft

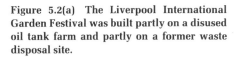
Figure 5.2(a) The Liverpool International Garden Festival was built partly on a disused oil tank farm and partly on a former waste disposal site.

Figure 5.2(b) The stability of the pavillion at the Liverpool International Garden Festival was ensured very simply by removal of the refuse in this area of the site.

pockets. Light loads can be carried by appropriate raft foundations. Heavier loads may require a special investigation of the site and more elaborate foundations.

In old housing areas one of the major problems is the old services. These will have to be found and relocated in relation to new site plans. Old sewers have to be filled in accordance with legislation. Roadways may have to be removed. Foundations need not cause a problem for new houses provided that their foundations are taken to the depth of any earlier foundations. Otherwise the old foundations must be removed. Old cellars can present a problem which can only be dealt with if each cellar is excavated and properly refilled. Since larger structures require deeper foundations, previously buildings will rarely cause problems for large developments, as is demonstrated by all the redevelopment that has taken place in our cities.

Derelict land must be used more and more for building development. The most crucial step is the site investigation. Once this has been done effectively, new developments can proceed with confidence. Many of the present difficulties could be avoided in the future by the closer control of materials and placing techniques, the keeping of adequate records at tipping sites likely to be used as building land and the retention of plans of buildings especially where these are large and have complex foundations. A site which has been swept clean in the interests of tidiness, and for which no plans for the former buildings remain, is always likely to give problems.

5.4 Disposing of wastes

We now produce 100 million tonnes of domestic and industrial wastes every year in England, which have to be disposed of. All are regulated by the requirements of the Deposit of Poisonous Wastes Act and the Control of Pollution Act, which ensure safe and sensible disposal. But it does not determine the final land-use and reclamation, which require as much thought and care as in any mining operation. Mining land and derelict land can make an important contribution to the disposal of wastes. Hazardous wastes have considerable potential problems and have to be disposed of carefully. Non-toxic industrial wastes and domestic refuse, in contrast, are much easier to dispose of and can be of great value to derelict

Figure 5.3   Quarries and other derelict sites can provide important sites for the disposal of wastes; a disused railway cutting at Bluntisham Heath, Cambridgeshire, filled with domestic refuse and restored to agriculture.

Figure 5.4   The restoration of waste disposal sites must be carried out with care, otherwise the escaping methane gas may kill the vegetation.

land reclamation, as landfill, on which crops or grass can be established after treatment.

The word 'landfill' tends to imply something rather benign, which is not necessarily true. Many wastes are high in organic matter – because of packaging materials domestic refuse is now more than 60% organic. This decomposes and in the absence of oxygen produces a mixture of gases including methane which is not only inflammable but also can kill deep rooting plants, especially trees, by depriving their roots of oxygen. The production of landfill gas may persist for many years. These problems can be overcome where agricultural soils are replaced over refuse, by covering the refuse first with an impermeable layer, normally of clay. This acts as a barrier to the upward diffusion of the gases which must then be vented away by pipes and burnt or dispersed harmlessly into the air at special outlets. This is not difficult to arrange if it is done at the time when the waste is being covered (see Case Study 6.8).

The second problem is consolidation and shrinkage. Many wastes are organic and contain air spaces. With the passage of time the organic matter and the spaces disappear and the waste may reduce substantially in volume, by as much as 50%. Modern wastes tend to shrink more than older ones which mostly consisted of household ash. The situation has been greatly improved by the development of special machines, compactors, which spread and consolidate the material in one operation. However, shrinkage of at least two metres in ten must still be expected. To allow for this the ground can be domed accordingly. Although, therefore, there are excellent final uses for waste disposal sites, the choice is rather limited (see Table 7.1).

In the future it may well be sensible to follow the German example and concentrate the rubbish into 'rubbish mountains' which, when properly treated, can be positive additions to the landscape. Whatever happens the siting of waste disposal sites must take into account the nature of the surrounding land and land uses, and the final land use must be determined at the outset.

5.5 Establishing vegetation

Many of the most practicable treatments for waste land involve the establishment of some kind of vegetation. This can be something productive, such as an agricultural crop, or something that is established merely to give a green cover. To do either it is necessary to make the land suitable for plants to grow properly. This may seem difficult, but the requirements of plants are really very straightforward and not difficult to satisfy, providing a reasonable soil can be provided or produced. On neglected land the original soil will usually be present, although perhaps in poor condition. This can easily be improved by normal agricultural and horticultural techniques.

On derelict land, however, there will usually be little or no soil present. To restore this land the simplest solution is to bring in the top soil from elsewhere. By doing this all the soil problems are overcome in one operation. It is a very simple, effective solution which is widely used. It is most used where there is no soil-forming material at all to start with and a productive soil is required, for instance, for allotments or high grade agriculture. However, the solution does have problems. Firstly, it is usually very expensive, up to £15,000 per hectare, because the soil has to be carried in from somewhere else, and secondly, it may be difficult to find soil of reasonable quality. The soil has to be laid without being damaged similarly to immediate land restoration procedures (see Chapter 3).

It is now common to make a new soil out of the materials that occur on

Table 5.2 The underlying problems of derelict land and their treatment

			Immediate treatment	Long-term treatment
Physical				
	Structure	Too compact	Rip or scarify	Vegetation
		Too open	Compact or cover with fine material	Vegetation
	Stability	Unstable	Stabilizer/mulch	Regrade or vegetation
	Moisture	Too wet	Drain	Drain
		Too dry	Organic mulch	Vegetation
Nutrition				
	Macronutrients	Nitrogen	Fertilizer	Legume
		Others	Fertilizer + lime	Fertilizer + lime
	Micronutrients		Fertilizer	–
Toxicity				
	pH	Too high	Pyritic waste or organic matter	Weathering
		Too low	Lime	Lime
	Heavy metals	Too high	Organic mulch or metal tolerant cultivar	Inert covering or metal tolerant cultivar
	Salinity	Too high	Weathering or irrigate	Tolerant species or cultivar

Figure 5.5 Legumes, like white clover, are an important tool in land reclamation, because of the nitrogen they can contribute to the soil.

Figure 5.6 Soil compaction can be overcome by modern ripping machinery.

site. This means correcting the individual problems and deficiencies of the site materials. The main ways in which the materials may be unsuitable are (i) physical characters, which may prevent the plants rooting properly, (ii) nutritional characteristics, which may mean there is a deficiency of the important plant nutrients such as nitrogen, phosphorus and potassium, and (iii) toxicity, where there may be high acidity or alkalinity, or levels of toxic metals, sufficient to kill or injure any plants which try to grow. Modern scientific research has worked out a range of effective treatments most of which are inexpensive (Table 5.2).

It is obviously necessary to know what is wrong with the land before it can be put right. This will be provided by the initial survey. Then it may be necessary to set up greenhouse or field experiments to confirm the exact treatments which will be most effective. There are good accounts now of the way to set up these kind of trials, and detailed considerations of how individual problems can be treated, in a number of general and technical publications, details of which are given in Appendix 1. However, attention should be paid to the way some particularly common problems can be overcome.

(a) *Agricultural crops*

It is crucial to obtain a very good soil structure. The subsoil and top soil must have a good structure, achieved by choosing the right type of material and careful preparation by ripping and surface cultivation. The top soil must contain adequate organic matter as a store for plant nutrients and to encourage good biological activity. This can best be done by establishing first a grass and legume mixture. Some organic wastes, such as sewage sludge, can be very valuable amendments. Sufficient lime and fertiliser must be added at the outset and to each year's crop, taking into account the special deficiencies of the soil-forming material. It is always difficult to restore waste land to highly productive agricultural land, but there have been some remarkable successes, as with pulverised fuel ash from power stations.

(b) *Grass*

Grass can be established on a much wider range of materials – almost anything from coarse sand to heavy clay. The initial soil structure is less important, so long as it is good enough for the seed to establish; the grass is a long term improver. Grass requires a balanced nutrient supply to start with, provided by an appropriate fertiliser. Later, a long term supply of nitrogen is necessary, nitrogen always being deficient in derelict land. This is best achieved by including white clover *(Trifolium repens)*, or other legumes, in the seeds mixture which can transfer large amounts of nitrogen from the air to plant growth, by nitrogen-fixing bacteria on their roots. With this approach, even very unattractive sites, like urban clearance areas, can be treated extremely simply and cheaply.

(c) *Forestry*

Trees require a loose, uncompacted soil. There are now machines developed by the Forestry Commission which enable the soil to be ripped and thoroughly broken up to a depth of almost a metre. These allow materials, such as the basement beds left after working for sand and gravel, to be transformed into a suitable medium for tree planting. Trees also require an adequate supply of nutrients especially nitrogen and phosphorus. Where nitrogen is deficient, nitrogen-fixing trees and shrubs, such as alder and tree lupin, can be planted in mixtures with other species.

(d) *Amenity trees and shrubs*

These are commonly planted on derelict and neglected land because of the great contribution they can make to the landscape. It is imperative that they are given the proper treatment, if they are to establish quickly. It is better to use small transplants or whips rather than large standards except where an immediate effect is essential. The soil must be satisfactory for plant growth in terms of its structure and nutrient content. A good soil should be kept for tree and shrub planting, and a poor soil can be amended with appropriate fertilisers. If the trees are large and have to be staked, this must be done with care and the ties checked and adjusted every year.

Figure 5.7 Disused railway lines can find new uses with very little treatment; the Monsal Trail at Chee Dale in the Peak District National Park.

5.6 Wildlife and nature conservation

On many older sites wild life has colonised so well that they are interesting and valuable for nature conservation and therefore require very little extra treatment (see Case Study 6.12.) All that may be needed is to establish paths and nature trails, and to control access particularly to prevent rubbish dumping. There are many younger sites however, that have great potential, such as quarries, flooded gravel pits or urban wasteland, whose natural development requires assistance. This can involve little more than the introduction of ecologically appropriate plants, but it may be necessary to substantially reshape the materials to create the right underlying landforms. Using these two in combination, some remarkable sites combining nature conservation and amenity, such as at Great Linford (Case Study 6.9) and Sevenoaks, have been made where not only plants but also animals and birds prosper greatly. Many of these sites can end up much more beautiful in their new state than they were originally.

But in some sites there is a more precise requirement – to put back the original vegetation. Obviously a virgin woodland whose history goes back thousands of years can never be restored, which is a strong argument for preserving those which remain. But modern techniques do allow us to put back many sorts of wild vegetation by very careful stripping of the soil and plants and their rapid reinstatement afterwards. This is most possible in a progressive operation such as a pipeline where there are now some remarkable examples.

Figure 5.8 With care it is possible to restore completely the original natural vegetation of a site; a gas pipeline runs away into the distance from the bottom centre of this photograph.

5.7 Contaminated land

Unfortunately, some derelict land may be contaminated with poisonous substances produced by past industries such as gas works and metal refining. There are also heaps of waste produced by bygone mining for lead, zinc and copper. These sites often show their toxicity by their bareness and lack of plants. They must be treated with caution and careful site surveys carried out by specialists before any work is commenced. If the level of contamination is not too high, simple treatments to establish grass and trees may be possible.

If the toxic material is likely to cause a health hazard, it may either have to be removed and buried in a licensed disposal site or left where it is and in some manner isolated from its potential targets. Very successful barriers can often be made from other wastes which are not toxic, occurring on the site, or from unwanted local materials such as subsoils from a building site or quarry wastes as at Parc Mine (Case Study 6.13). Alternatively, industrial buildings, roadways or parking areas can be constructed.

In many cases the contamination is restricted to some parts of the site and the other parts can be given simple treatments and restored to a demanding land use such as agriculture or residential housing with gardens as at Willow Tree Lane (Case Study 6.3). Useful published guidelines and descriptions for the treatment of toxic sites are now available (see Appendix I).

5.8 Aftercare

The restoration of derelict and neglected land cannot ever be completed in one step or in one season. The plants and soils take time to develop and mature into self-sustaining systems. As a result, aftercare of reclaimed sites is always essential, indeed, it is as crucial as all the previous work. Fertilisers and manures will be important to assist the build-up of fertility and encourage the growth of legumes. Trees and other plants will need tending. Until plants are established, weed control will be important. Any possible recurrence of toxicity will have to be monitored. General growth itself may be monitored. Agricultural yields have to be properly recorded. Careful experimentation will reveal the aftercare treatments most necessary. If aftercare is built into the final land use management of the site, it need not be costly.

5.9 A successful restoration programme

There are, therefore, a number of steps that have to be taken if the restoration of any site is to be both successful and economical. A flow chart for the work is shown in Figure 5.9. The programmes are very similar whether a hard or a soft end use is intended. Each stage involves proper technical input. A successful programme must make use of the scientific and technical skills which are now readily available to guide and sharpen what is to be done. With these, land restoration and developments can be effective and economical; without them it can be second-rate and expensive.

Transforming our Waste Land: The Way Forward

Figure 5.9   Flow chart for the work required for successful site reclamation.

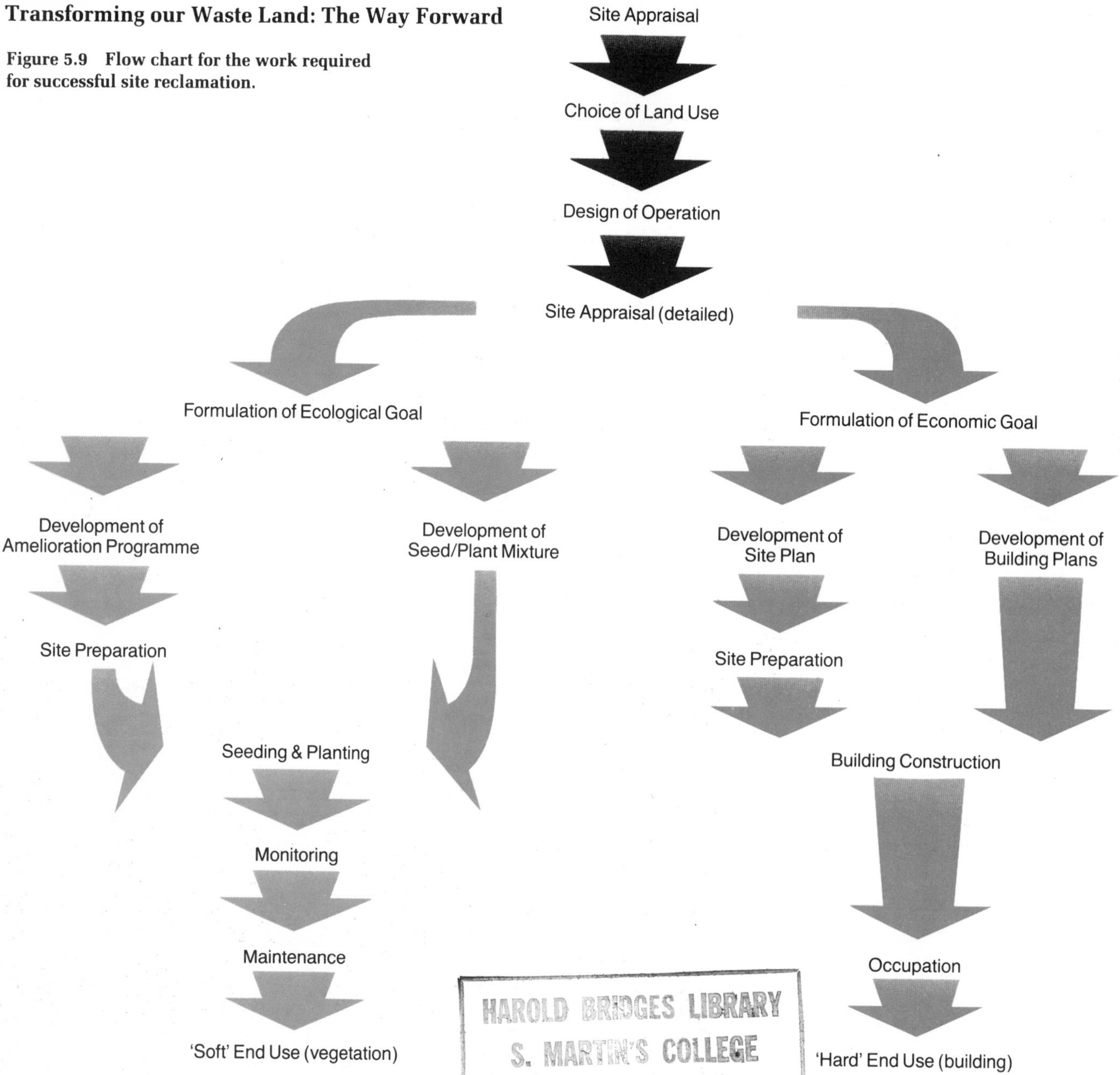

Site Appraisal

Choice of Land Use

Design of Operation

Site Appraisal (detailed)

Formulation of Ecological Goal

Formulation of Economic Goal

Development of
Amelioration Programme

Development of
Seed/Plant Mixture

Development of
Site Plan

Development of
Building Plans

Site Preparation

Site Preparation

Seeding & Planting

Monitoring

Maintenance

'Soft' End Use (vegetation)

Building Construction

Occupation

'Hard' End Use (building)

Chapter 6

Case Histories

6.1 Urban wet area to amenity

Figure 6.1a An old dam at St. Helens which used to provide water for the chemical industry, cleaned and restored by a combination of a local action group, St. Helens Metropolitan District Council and the Groundwork Trust.

SUTTON MILL DAM, ST. HELENS

Sutton Mill Dam was established in the eighteenth century to power a local corn mill. In the next century water was abstracted for use in glass manufacture and later for the chemical industry. As time went on the dam silted up and its industrial value declined to the point where its use for waste disposal was contemplated by the owner. This produced a strong reaction from local residents who formed an Action Group. The local authority, St. Helens Borough Council, resisted waste disposal and, having acquired the Dam, came forward with proposals for interim recreational use. The local residents, however, proposed a more natural solution which has now been adopted by the Borough Council. The Residents Action Group is still active and they recognised that the key to successful reclamation was sympathetic use of the area by future generations.

Figure 6.1b The Nature Pack which was specially developed for the area being officially presented to a local primary school.

With this in mind they commissioned the Groundwork Trust in St. Helens to produce a nature pack about the Dam for use by local primary schools. The trio of The Groundwork Trust, the Borough Council and the Action Group, working in partnership has produced a reclamation scheme which is tailored to the needs of the community. This involves sympathetic treatment of the dam wall to ensure it copes with flood conditions, dredging of open water areas, retention of natural vegetation around the water, preservation of a swampy area as a wildlife habitat and introduction of foothpaths and board walks to provide access around and across the dam. This scheme is costing substantially less than a conventional restoration scheme to implement, and, more importantly, reduces the long term maintenance costs substantially.

6.2 Urban area to industrial development

KINGSWAY LOOP, LIVERPOOL

The construction in the mid 1970's of the approach to the second Mersey Tunnel crossing provided a classic example of an area of approximately 5 acres of land which had, on three occasions in the past, been intensively developed and redeveloped, and was now isolated from the remainder of the City by the deep cut of the Tunnel approach roads. Access was provided by means of one heavy duty bridge but this had remained unused for 7 years.

New development had not taken place during the period due to the high cost of constructing foundations on a site covered with the remains of the old basements, ground beams, roadworks, in some cases extending back several hundred years. The ownership of the site was jointly divided between Merseyside County Council and Liverpool City Council.

The familiar pattern of a major company rationalisation occurred when Whitbreads closed their existing breweries in both Birkenhead and Liverpool following the opening of the new Samsbury complex in the greenbelt between Preston and Blackburn. It provided the company with the opportunity of constructing its new regional distribution depot, either in the Warrington New Town Motorway box, or remain in the Liverpool City Centre thus retaining the balance of 300 existing jobs within the City. Company executives were persuaded to remain, on the basis of a high profile site located on a major motor access both into the City Centre and into the motorway system.

Figure 6.2 A significant area in Liverpool at the entrance to one of the Mersey tunnels, reclaimed for industrial use by a private developer with the aid of a substantial Urban Development Grant.

Design problems arose from the building of 110,000 square feet having heavy duty storage of beers which necessitated careful foundation design in the difficult ground conditions, complicated by the high retaining walls to the loop roadworks.

The Liverpool Task Force section of the Department of Environment provided an Urban Development Grant to cover extra costs above normal 'greenfield' cost conditions. Thus the £2·25 million project was completed on time within 8 months. The developers state that without such a grant from the Task Force it would have been non-viable to carry out the building works, and thus the Whitbread company would have moved from the City Centre with the subsequent loss of 300 jobs to Liverpool.

6.3 Urban waste to housing and open space

WILLOW TREE LANE, WEST LONDON

The Willow Tree Lane Joint Development is situated in West London within the London Boroughs of Hillingdon and Ealing. The site is 65 hectares in area. Although the site was agricultural until 1895, it was subsequently used for brickmaking with the resultant voids filled by domestic refuse tipped to heights of 11m above ground. At one stage it was receiving 43,000 tons of refuse annually, delivered by canal barge. Refuse tipping ceased in 1950.

The land was acquired from private landowners by a consortium of the London Borough of Hillingdon, the Greater London Council and the

Figure 6.3a The Willow Tree Lane site in West London before reclamation. Originally a brick pit which was later filled with domestic refuse, it was found to contain high levels of lead, mercury, cadmium and salt.

Figure 6.3b Modern houses, shops and schools are being built on the site after removal of contaminated material. The rest of the area is set out as a spacious public park.

London Borough of Ealing. A planning brief was published, demonstrating the potential of the site to provide 1600 homes with schools, shops, community buildings and substantial public open space, including playing fields and provision for an athletics track.

Extensive site investigations found that, of the site area of 65 hectares, 43 were contaminated. A major series of site investigations showed high levels of salt concentrations present, along with lead, cadmium and mercury. A substantial chicken manure pit was also discovered. Tests were carried out for methane, asbestos, non-metallic contaminants, combustion, corrosion and general groundwater contaminations. Final reclamation proposals were drawn up by Brian Clouston and Partners, based on the results of the extensive programme.

An initial reclamation contract was let in July 1977 to clear large areas of the site for development and to create the principal public open space. 3 hectares on the west of the site was cleared of contaminated material in order to create building sites, and this material was reused in recontouring the eastern contaminated areas. The remaining 40 hectares of contaminated land did not affect the structure plan layout; the 21 uncontaminated hectares were to be developed for building purposes.

This first contract was followed by others, for drainage, service

infrastructure, landscape and public open space in connection with schools and housing, and a new bridge over the Grand Union Canal adjacent to the site. The scheme is continuing, with housing being developed on the site and the initial landscape infrastructure developing into a maturing benefit for the whole community.

A particular concern now is the long term maintenance of the scheme. Hillingdon appears unable to find the resources to cut significant weed growth under trees, replant transplants in selected areas, or thin out trees in exceptionally successful areas to reinforce planting in other areas. At the same time they have cut all wild seed areas on banks and meadows creating significantly more work for their stretched resources. This would indicate a failure of understanding on principles of landscape maintenance, despite extensive discussions held during design and implementation. This problem could be avoided if maintenance was controlled and managed by the initial design team for 5 years in a period of 'aftercare', as already recognised as being necessary in minerals act legislation. Aftercare can then be geared towards specific long term goals and not seen simply as a means of keeping grounds staff employed.

6.4 Urban site to wildlife refuge

RACQUETS CLUB, UPPER PARLIAMENT STREET, LIVERPOOL

The building on this site was destroyed during the Toxteth riots of 1981. It was a gentleman's club having its origins in the slave-trading merchants of Liverpool. The site was derelict and a mess and there was an urgent need to make it look attractive at low cost, so that it could be held, in a land bank, for later development. The remaining walls and other structures were crushed into the former basement areas of the club and the site levelled. As a result, the substrate of the site was building rubble about 4m deep. The site was bare, without any colonising vegetation at time of treatment.

The site was designed by the Rural Preservation Association to have three zones of vegetation, woodland edge, meadow and close-mown grass, to give diversity and opportunity for wild life. Areas to be planted with trees were topsoiled to a depth of about 15cm (6 inches) and planted with attractive native species, oak, ash, willow, crab apple, blackthorn, hawthorn, guelder rose, but also with London plane trees to match a similar planting on a site opposite.

The establishment of herbaceous vegetation was based on the principle that urban wasteland on brick rubble tends to be well-drained, reasonably fertile with the exception of nitrogen, and quite calcareous. The site was therefore sown with a fescue grass mix without the addition of fertiliser, and with birds-foot trefoil, a native legume of neutral and calcareous grasslands, included in the seed mix to increase N levels. Other grassland and wasteland herbs that were introduced included chicory, mullein and mallow. In future years, as the fertility increases, more meadow perennials will be introduced to the grassland to establish an interesting wild flower area on an inner-city wasteland site progressively and at low cost without the use of fertiliser and very little topsoil. The economic benefits of a scrub and meadow treatment are obvious, both in terms of avoiding large-scale topsoil use and in reduced maintenance.

The scrub needs no management except occasional litter collection; a chicory-sown grassed area needs no maintenance in the early years of

Figure 6.4   The Racquets Club in Liverpool was destroyed by fire in 1981. A low cost revegetation of the rubble has been carried out by the Rural Preservation Association using native plant species.
before restoration work began *(above),*
good establishment of shrubs and chicory (left foreground), the grass verges next to the path have been mown *(right).*

establishment except for the removal of dead vegetation in winter. If the scrub invades it later, this will not matter. At the same time the whole area will become an increasing haven for wild life, especially birds, as the herbaceous vegetation develops and seeds, and the shrubs flower and set fruit.

The scheme was funded with a 100% Derelict Land Grant from the Department of the Environment.

6.5 Colliery spoil heaps to agriculture with the aid of an interim washery operation

THORNLEY COLLIERY, CO. DURHAM

Closure of the colliery at Thornley, Co. Durham, left not only the colliery buildings derelict but also a large coal washing plant serving several local pits, and a massive colliery spoil tip which dominated surrounding villages. Reclamation was undertaken by Durham County Council in two phases. The pit heaps were treated in a first phase during 1973/74. The central washery continued serving other local collieries until 1977, when it too was closed and subsequently reclaimed by the County Council in the second phase of the works. During the intervening period, the National Coal Board placed all the discarded material from the washery to contours agreed with the County Council, which therefore reduced considerably the costs of the bulk earthmoving necessary to achive a satisfactory land form.

In order to treat the 58 hectares of derelict land, 8 hectares of peripheral degraded land was included in the scheme. This provided not only spreading space but also valuable topsoil and subsoil which was spread thinly over selected parts of the new land form. The costs of acquisition (£17,000) and of reclamation (£311,000) (mid 1970 prices) were met by Derelict Land Grant from the Department of the Environment. As a result of reclamation, the site now consists of 47 hectares of pasture, 12 hectares of woodland and 7 hectares of public open space. Local farmers occupy the fields under seasonal licences which allow the harvesting of a hay crop followed by grazing by sheep or cows until the end of October each year. Both grass yields and licence fees approach levels expected from good land in the locality. An Angling Club now leases a pond which was developed on the site and there are also allotments. As a result, the total gross income from the site is in the region of £8,600 per annum. The net income is about £1,400. Similar techniques have been used on most of the

2,350 hectares of derelict land treated by the County Council. If the land is properly managed after reclamation, the long term success of these schemes, in terms of finance, as well as reclamation, seems assured.

Figure 6.5 The reclamation of the old colliery site at Thornley was simplified by the operation of a coal washery; the discarded material from this was carefully placed to minimise the need for earth moving in the final restoration to agriculture.
1973 before restoration *(above)*,
1980 after restoration has been completed and the land is in good production *(below)*.

6.6 Opencast coal to agriculture

ALBERT OPENCAST COAL SITE, HINDLEY, GREATER MANCHESTER

Before being mined, the Albert opencast coal site consisted of former Albert Colliery site including tips and stocking grounds, a subsidence pond known as Diggle Flash and agricultural land including some marsh and sparse woodland. During the opencast mining 740,000 tonnes of good quality coal was won from 38 hectares, the remainder of the 79 hectare site being used for overburden dumps, soil dumps, access, internal roads and a coal disposal plant. Before the coal could be removed, first the topsoil,

Figure 6.6 The Albert opencast coal site is typical of the many areas worked for coal and rapidly restored to agriculture and public open space.
during extraction *(above),*
after restoration *(below).*

then the subsoil, had to be carefully stripped and separately stored. Then the overburden overlying the coal was excavated.

Restoration was progressive and involved backfilling the overburden followed by first the replacement of the subsoil and then the topsoil. 16 hectares in the north western part of the site is to be used as public open space, the rest of the site will be available for agriculture.

After topsoiling, a temporary grass seed mix was sown, mostly perennial rye grass *(Lolium perenne)* and white clover *(Trifolium repens)*. In the first two years the site was underdrained, fenced and hedgerows and trees planted. It was then reseeded with a permanent grass mixture. During the early stages, use of the land was restricted to a hay crop only so that the newly replaced soil would not be damaged.

Once the rehabilitation of the land is completed the local authority will take over the 16 hectares of public open space. The remainder will go into full time agricultural production. Not only will good agricultural land have been completely reinstated, but a disused area of operational land associated with the Albert Colliery put back to the agricultural land it had been a century ago.

6.7 Former sewage works to housing and public park

BARNS LANE, WALSALL

This project for the reclamation of a sixteen acre former sewage works, to provide three acres of residential development land and a thirteen acre local park, was given Category A status for Derelict Land Grant by the Department of the Environment.

The land was acquired by West Midlands County Council in March 1984 for about £120,000 and reclamation works started immediately. In order to eliminate the lead time required for normal contractual procedures and to simplify the ultimate disposal of the reclaimed development land, the scheme was implemented utilising the County Council's Annual Tender for the Hire of Plant and Equipment.

Necessary works in the housing area included the removal of heavy, concrete, sub-surface installations, and sewage sludge, as well as excavation, regrading and compaction to suit the intended development. In the parkland, the sewage works installations were appropriately dealt with, and a small new lake, complete with nesting island, was constructed. Excavated spoil from the new lake met the shortfall of fill material on what

Figure 6.7 When the former sewage works at Barns Lane became redundant, West Midlands County Council acquired the land and carried out reclamation work with the aid of a Derelict Land Grant under the Category A Scheme. From the sale of part of the site for housing it expects to cover the cost of the whole reclamation.
aerial view before reclamation *(above)*,
the site today *(below).*

had been a flat site, and permitted the ground to be re-modelled to add interest to the new park. An area of naturally regenerated scrubland at the north eastern side was retained. The total cost of this work was about £95,000.

Works in the development area were given precedence and were completed during July 1984. In the same month, following a prior agreement, the housing land was sold to Tarmac Homes (Midlands), and construction commenced forthwith, the first dwellings being occupied before Christmas 1984. It is anticipated that landscape works on the parkland will be completed during 1985.

On this Category A land reclamation project the total acquisition and works costs are expected to be closely matched by the sale value of the housing land.

6.8 Sand and gravel quarry returned to agriculture after refuse disposal

HATFIELD QUARRY, HERTFORDSHIRE

Throughout the lowlands, sand and gravel workings are common wherever there are suitable deposits, to provide materials for the construction industry. Many of these deposits are extensive but shallow, in river valleys, and covered with excellent surface soils. As a result, the agricultural value of the land is often Grade 1 or 2 on the official agricultural land classification. The great need in these areas is to return the land to agriculture without any loss of productivity.

But the removal of perhaps 5-10 metres of sand and gravel means that the land surface is lowered, so making difficulties for drainage. It is therefore possible to fill the empty workings with household or industrial wastes before restoration, by which not only can the original levels be restored, but a useful extra income derived.

This was the situation at the Hatfield Quarry of St. Albans Sand and Gravel , previously 32ha of Grade 2 agricultural land used for a wide variety of arable crops. From the earliest stages topsoil and subsoil have been removed and replaced after extraction. The technique now operating involves a number of simple but important steps, each of which is crucial, to ensure that the restoration is successful.

The topsoil and subsoil were carefully stripped and stored separately under dry conditions so they were neither lost nor damaged. After the sand and gravel had been removed, the void was filled with imported industrial waste spread in well-compacted thin layers to a domed shape, which allowed for shrinkage and drainage. Perforated pipes were then inserted into the surface of the fill to allow any methane gas generated by decomposition of the waste to vent away. The surface was then covered with a clay seal, and the original subsoil and topsoil carefuly respread under dry conditions.

The soil was then ripped thoroughly to ensure that there was no compaction. A land drainage system was inserted, the topsoil sown to grass and fertilised carefully. Arable cropping only began after three or four years. The procedure of sowing grass first and wheat later is not always carried out. St. Albans Sand and Gravel are currently monitoring sites which have been initially seeded with winter wheat.

The results for the arable cropping have been excellent. The yields of winter wheat in 1984 for the first two fields restored have been 8.42 and 7.96 tonnes per ha. A rough estimate for the Hatfield Parish mean yields in 1984 for the same crop was 7.25 tonnes per hectare. The figures speak for themselves.

Figure 6.8 The Hatfield quarry is a good example of land from which minerals have been won, household refuse disposed of and wheat harvested.
wastes covered and gas venting system being laid *(left),*
8 tonnes of winter wheat per hectare *(right).*

6.9 Sand and gravel pit to water and wildlife

GREAT LINFORD, BUCKINGHAMSHIRE

Great Linford pit has been an important source of sand and gravel for the construction industry since shortly after the Second World War. From it Amey Roadstone has produced almost 10 million tonnes of aggregate. The site is 300 hectares in the flood plain of the upper reaches of the Great Ouse river, 2 km west of Newport Pagnell in North Buckinghamshire and immediately to the north of Milton Keynes. Because it tends to fill naturally with water and is located near to a new town, it seemed sensible that the after-use of the pit should be largely leisure-orientated. The operation itself has produced considerable quantities of overburden which has allowed partial infilling of the pits. As a result, sizeable tracts of land as well as water remained after mineral working. This has been an advantage since it has allowed more interesting contouring of the land being restored.

Restoration is carried out progressively, following closely behind extraction. A working party, including production, lands management,

Figure 6.9 Where sand and gravel is extracted from low lying areas, sizeable tracts of land and water may be produced, which at Great Linford are being landscaped into a variety of end uses including sailing and wildlife.

landscaping and Game Conservancy specialists, which was set up to plan the final end uses of the site, has aimed at developing a leisure area focussed on 200ha of water created as extraction proceeds. This includes fishing and sailing facilities, picnic and walking areas, camping and an arboretum. At the same time some land is being returned to agriculture and some is being afforested. But the site provides another, rather unique after-use, as a wildfowl centre. As soon as excavation of the Great Linford complex of pits was started, it began to be used by relatively large numbers of wintering birds. The lake and surroundings within the complex, which had the best potential was therefore selected as the site for the centre and is being developed both as a breeding sanctuary as well as a winter refuge, financed by Amey Roadstone Corporation and managed by the Game Conservancy. In the Wildfowl Reserve area, farm animals have been excluded and the shorelines have been carefully graded and planted with native wetland plants with help from the British Trust for Conservation Volunteers. 145 species of birds have been recorded at the site since 1972, of which 80 are known to have bred in the study area.

A research laboratory, conference room and associated leisure facilities and a workshop have been built. In addition to the research function, the centre is also an important educational unit. Parties of school children, university students, naturalists, planning authorities, quarry operators and overseas visitors continually visit the site, both to study the wildfowl and to see how the same idea can be translated to other sites.

Great Linford provides an excellent example of how careful planning can ensure that mineral-bearing land which was used in the construction of a new city, Milton Keynes, can be turned to a completely new use as an area of recreation, quiet enjoyment and nature conservation.

6.10 Hard rock quarry restored to agriculture

MOOTLAW QUARRY, NORTHUMBERLAND

Mootlaw Quarry is situated 10 miles north east of Hexham, Northumberland and is operated by North Tyne Roadstone, a company jointly owned by Amey Roadstone and Tarmac.

The quarry is working the Great Limestone which forms the basal unit of the Upper Limestone Group of the Lower Carboniferous System. The deposit has a thickness of up to 17 metres and the series dips eastwards at about 5°. This configuration allows restoration of the relatively shallow

Figure 6.10 Restoration of a limestone quarry floor to agriculture while mineral working is still proceeding; Mootlaw Quarry, Northumberland.

working to proceed on the floor of the quarry. The soil and overburden overlying the deposit is separately stripped and stored during excavation of the limestone and is used for final restoration. The floor of the quarry is firstly covered with 2 metres of quarry waste or scalpings, which provide both the necessary fall and drainage to the site. The overburden and soil is then replaced in the relevant order and the land restored to its previous agricultural use.

Restoration is of a high standard and produces high yielding grass crops. This is achieved through excellent co-operation between the land owner, who also farms the land, the operator and the Northumberland County Council, assisted by advice from the Ministry of Agriculture, Fisheries and Food.

6.11 Chemical waste to golf course

Figure 6.11a **Extremely inhospitable chemical wastes at Widnes.**

Figure 6.11b **After landscaping, covering the wastes with an inert material and establishing vegetation, an attractive and much-needed golf course has been created.**

ST. MICHAEL'S JUBILEE GOLF COURSE, WIDNES

Widnes was the starting place of the British heavy chemical industry. As a result, by the 1960's it was ringed round with waste heaps produced in the days when there were no planning controls for waste disposal. This particular site was 31 ha of mixed, unstable, chemical wastes from various sources. Fifty years of copper refining and associated waste disposal resulted in some 10 ha of the tip being seriously contaminated with copper, zinc and cadmium and even barium, posing considerable environmental problems. Obviously many possible after-uses were precluded. On closure of the works the waste tip area was therefore acquired by the local authority, Halton Borough Council and redeveloped as a golf course, in collaboration with the County Council, to provide a much-needed amenity for the area.

The concentration of copper was well in excess of 1%. This, together with a variety of other heavy metals, resulted in a surface which was extremely inhospitable to plant growth. In this sort of situation the only permanent solution is to provide a deep covering of an inert material to act as a barrier isolating the chemical wastes from the restored surface.

On the same site, there were large quantities of the waste product of the local soda ash industry, consisting largely of calcium hydroxide and calcium sulphide. This alkaline material was used to provide a 0.5 m cover over the metal-contaminated waste. The high alkalinity of the cover material in itself will inhibit plant growth, but will reduce the solubility of the metals in the original waste and reduce their potential for movement. The grass required for the golf course was then established by applying a thin layer of topsoil (150mm) over the lime waste. The whole site has been carefully landscaped and groups of trees planted in pockets of deeper soil. The acquisition and reclamation costs were £207,212 (85% DoE grant aid), enhancement and club house costs were £481,650. Job Creation programme costs were £15,502. The reclamation was commenced in 1964 and carried out in stages. Enough land was reclaimed to begin with to make a 9 hole golf course. This was subsequently enlarged to allow an 18 hole course to be completed by 1983.

6.12 Chemical waste to wildlife

NOB END, FARNWORTH, NEAR BOLTON, GREATER MANCHESTER

The Nob End site at Farnworth was occupied during the last century by a chemical factory which produced sodium carbonate (soda-ash) by the Leblanc process. This produced vast quantities of toxic alkali waste contaminated with calcium sulphides and other chemicals.

The Leblanc works closed around the turn of the century, leaving about 9.5 hectares of derelict chemical wasteland. During the last 80 years or so the surface material has been washed free of toxic alkali by rainfall, leaving a lime-rich friable soil. This has been colonised naturally by lime-loving plants such as wild orchids and other unusual and attractive species.

Much of the site, however, was covered with boiler ash, demolition rubble, subsoil and other materials. This supported a sparse acidic flora or unattractive weedy vegetation with bare ground in places.

Originally it was intended to reclaim the site to agriculture, which would have involved costly engineering works, soil importation and cultivation. In view of the natural history of parts of the site it was decided to reclaim it for informal public open space and wildlife uses, thereby conserving the wild orchid flora.

The only engineering work was the removal of a layer of acidic boiler ash to uncover lime waste for further natural colonisation by attractive orchids and other wild flowers. The boiler ash was used to infill depressions and holes in the ground. Parts of the site not covered with alkali waste were limed heavily, using 100 tonnes per hectare of ground limestone to promote the spread of orchids and lime-loving wild flowers over the majority of the site, site experiments having demonstrated that this could be done. Small areas of interesting acidic vegetation were left untreated to provide diversity and for study purposes.

Figure 6.12 During the last 80 years, the surface material of the alkali wastes at Nob End have been washed free of toxins by rainfall, leaving a lime-rich soil. A rich, calcium-loving flora including many orchids has colonised naturally in some areas and subsequent reclamation plans have taken the wildlife interests of the site into account.

Limited fencing work was carried out to exclude cattle and motorcycles which were damaging the natural flora. Gates and stiles were erected to allow public access.

The reclamation, completed in 1981, cost just over £13,000 including land acquisition and staff costs and was funded by a 100% Derelict Land Grant from the Department of the Environment. This was only £1,400 per hectare, demonstrating how reclamation costs can be drastically reduced by a policy of minimising the engineering works and improving the naturally established vegetation.

The scheme has been a great success. The wildlife interests of the site, particularly the orchid colonies and rare plants, have been conserved. Its appearance has been improved substantially as the attractive lime-loving plants have spread to the newly limed areas. Motor-cycle damage is no longer a problem. It is a most attractive wild area in a busy conurbation. Moreoever, the maintenance costs of the site are virtually nil, because fertilisation and grass cutting are unnecessary for wildlife and natural areas. All that is necessary is for the paths to be maintained.

6.13 Metalliferous mine waste stabilised and used for grazing

PARC MINE, LLANRWST, GWYNEDD

There are old lead/zinc mines scattered all over Britain, mined and then forgotten, leaving piles of wastes which, because of the metals they still contain, are some of the nastiest types of derelict land we have. Parc Mine near Llanrwst was one such example. When it finally closed in early 1960, it left behind a large unprotected heap of toxic waste containing as much as 0.8% lead and 1.0% zinc, poised in forest land up above the River Conway.

In 1964 thousands of tons of the waste were washed out in a storm and destroyed many hectares of high grade pasture in the valley below and polluted the whole river. Subsequent storms brought further waste down and the stream running beside the mine itself began to bite into the waste. In 1977 the Welsh Development Agency undertook major work to stabilise and reclaim it.

The problem was that because the waste was so toxic it was not going to be easy to grow plants directly on it. It was therefore decided to use an inert covering. Conveniently in a near-by quarry, itself derelict, was a large amount of inert waste, which because of its gravelly nature would make an

Figure 6.13a The waste heaps at Parc mine contain high levels of lead and zinc and their continual erosion was a threat to the Conway valley.

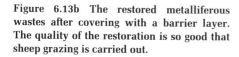

Figure 6.13b The restored metalliferous wastes after covering with a barrier layer. The quality of the restoration is so good that sheep grazing is carried out.

excellent barrier to the upward movement of metals from the waste below. This was spread over the site to a depth of 15 cms. No top soil cover was added, because it was decided that the barrier layer itself could be made fertile enough. A grass mixture was sown containing the special metal-tolerant variety of red fescue, 'Merlin', to make doubly sure there would be no problems. Heavy lime and fertilizer dressings were given.

The stream was diverted and canalised, and the drainage from the waste area itself passed through a limestone filter bed during the construction period to reduce metal pollution. As at Eyam (Case Study 6.14) the original intention was to leave the area alone afterwards, but the grass has grown so well and the barrier layer is restricting the upward movement of metals so effectively that grazing is now carried out.

The whole operation was costly because of the difficulties of the site, £400,000 for 3 hectares, paid by the Welsh Development Agency. But the wastes are no longer a threat.

6.14 Metalliferous wastes to agriculture without a soil cover

LAPORTE INDUSTRIES TAILINGS PONDS, NEAR EYAM, DERBYSHIRE

Metals, mainly lead and zinc, have been mined in the Peak District since Roman times. Because the methods of extraction were primitive, the wastes left behind often contained high levels of toxic metals and as a result have a patchy cover of vegetation which often includes specialised plants. The metals still cause problems for livestock.

The deposits often contain fluorspar, a very important industrial chemical. Mining for fluorspar, together with lead and zinc, has been

Figure 6.14a   A fluorspar tailings lagoon in Derbyshire.

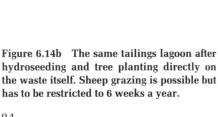

Figure 6.14b   The same tailings lagoon after hydroseeding and tree planting directly on the waste itself. Sheep grazing is possible but has to be restricted to 6 weeks a year.

carried out by Laporte Industries in Derbyshire for many years. The material comes from the surface and underground, is processed to extract the fluorspar and lead, and the finely ground wastes, or tailings, then have to be disposed of. This can only be done by depositing them in large lagoons, obviously a considerable imposition on the environment of a National Park and a potential source of toxicity.

To allow the important industry to continue, sites for these lagoons have had to be found, agreed with the planning authorities, in which the lagoon will have the least environmental impact. The lagoon walls are sited to be as self-effacing as possible, and grassed. The lagoons are then filled with tailings. Originally it was expected that nothing further could be done. But careful experiments showed that because of modern extraction techniques the wastes were not toxic to plants, and that grass legumes, and shrubs, could be grown if the fertility was built up with a combination of sewage sludge and fertilizers. In fact, the sewage sludge is used as a carrier for the seed so that it can be sprayed onto the surface of the tailings while they are still too soft to walk on – a technique known as hydroseeding.

Growth has been excellent. It was originally thought that levels of metals and fluoride in the foliage would be too high to permit grazing, and the area would be left for amenity. But the growth has been so good that there was pressure from the local farmers to graze it. Analysis showed that this was possible so long as the period of grazing was limited, as in some other parts of Derbyshire.

On the oldest lagoon, after 10 years the trees have formed patches of low woodland on the wind-swept site, and the sward is continuous, and it is very difficult to tell now that the sheep are grazing peacefully on what was once a tailings pond.

6.15 Sand waste tips rapidly covered with vegetation without the use of soil

LEE MOOR CHINA CLAY WORKINGS, DEVON

The china clay industry in South West England is an important contributor to our export trade. China clay deposits occur in certain specific places within the granites of both Cornwall and Devon as a result of ancient volcanic activity. The deposits are often very deep and most outcrop on the surface, and are worked as large open pits by hydraulic mining methods. The large deposits at Lee Moor lie within the edge of Dartmoor National Park.

The china clay itself constitutes only about one eighth of the material which is worked. The rest is waste, mostly coarse, gravelly sand, which cannot be put back into the pits until they are exhausted because it would obstruct further extraction. The waste must therefore be placed in large heaps on the surrounding land. Originally these heaps were conical, but with modern economical tipping methods they are now constructed in the form of long flat heaps rising in layers or lifts. In the Lee Moor area the sand tips amount to approximately 20 million tonnes. The wastes are not toxic but are very infertile.

Vegetation must be established directly on the sand waste as topsoil is either unavailable or unsuitable on the steep slopes of the tips. Long term research has shown that fertility can be increased with time if legumes are

Figure 6.15 The china clay sand waste heaps at Lee Moor on the edge of the Dartmoor National Park are being vegetated as part of a long term plan for the area, using techniques which allow grass and shrubs to be established directly on the waste.

present and regular inputs of lime and phosphate fertiliser are applied. The surfaces of the tips are sprayed with a slurry containing seed, fertiliser, lime and mulch. To obtain a stabilising and attractive cover rapidly, quick growing grasses are sown initially. These are followed up by a second sowing of perennial grasses and legumes. The legumes are very important because they build up the soil fertility. Where the grass is to be grazed, the legumes are mainly clovers, but where grazing is not envisaged, lupins are used because they require less management. Nevertheless, a careful regime of aftercare is carried out on all tips for at least ten years to ensure that fertility is built up satisfactorily.

There are now at least 100 hectares of tips treated in this way, many of them being grazed by sheep. Where appropriate for protection and for the landscape, trees are being planted. Initially the direct seeding technique has been applied to the new tips to cover them progressively as fast as they are being formed (Figure 3.7.). But older areas such as those shown here are now being tackled in relation to a long term landscape plan for the whole area of china clay workings.

6.16 Pulverised fuel ash tip to shopping and leisure complex

GATESHEAD METROCENTRE SCHEME

The Metrocentre site covers some 46ha of former agricultural water meadow on a flood plain of the river Tyne. Since the turn of the century this low-lying area has been extensively used for the storage of fly ash in conjunction with the operation of a sequence of power stations at Dunston and Stella. An indication of the poor condition of the site before reclamation and development commenced was given by Donaldson & Sons (Estate Agents & Valuers) in their Development and Marketing Report commissioned by Gateshead MBC and the Department of the Environment in 1982:

> "The present physical condition of the site presents a daunting prospect for a prospective developer, much of the site having been used for the storage of PFA, the various depths of which will have to be determined; lying in an area close to a river bed there will undoubtedly be alluvial deposits in the subsoil. Much of the site is wet with a large pond in the centre towards its northern edge. Various rough ditches are attempting to drain the site. There is a line

Figure 6.16a An explanatory view taken in 1982 of the Gateshead Metro site before development began; a waste land covered with fuel ash from the disused power station.

of pylons running within the site along the southern boundary and a second line diagonally along the site. The present access into the site is inadequate for any major redevelopment.''

Gateshead MBC and Tyne & Wear MCC together prepared alternative proposals for a public sector reclamation scheme for the site. Because of the technical complexities, expert advice was sought. Two reports proposed, following field trial recommendation, that the site should be reclaimed on the principle of rolling surcharge. Cameron Hall Developments adopted a modified scheme based on the recommendations. But owing to the scale of the proposals, investment had become such that piled main building foundations had become an economic proposition which had not originally been considered viable.

No public sector reclamation scheme has actually been undertaken. The developer, with the benefit of Enterprise Zone advantages, has undertaken all of the reclamation works using his own resources and the only publicly funded element is an Urban Development Grant application for a major interchange on the Western bypass trunk road which borders the southern boundary of the site. This is being funded by Gateshead MBC, Department of Transport and Department of the Environment.

Figure 6.16b The Gateshead Metro development in the summer of 1985.

Chapter 7   The Way Forward

Above all else it must be remembered that land is a scarce and non-renewable resource, the store of which is being constantly eroded. To overcome this we must make sure that we re-use land wherever it is possible.

It is very obvious, however, that we are not achieving a satisfactory level of land restoration in England. Both the amount of officially recorded derelict land and unofficial estimates of neglected land show that restoration of land is not even keeping pace with the appearance of new waste land. Why this situation should persist is not immediately obvious, as the benefits from reclaiming land are great. In its contribution to the 1972 United Nations Conference on the Human Environment held in Stockholm, the British Government made it clear that the need to improve the quality of life for a person should be a high priority for any authority, industry etc. with the power to do so. The World Conservation Strategy document produced in 1981 has been received favourably by Government. Ministers themselves have, on many occasions, shown considerable concern over the wasteland problem. It is quite clear that there is an urgent need to deal with the vast legacy of derelict and degraded land that has been inherited from previous generations and prevent further degradation occurring in the future. What then is the way forward?

7.1 The benefits of restoration

The most important principles that must be grasped are, firstly, there are many different possible end uses for the large amounts of wasteland in this country, and, secondly, that to bring these new uses into being does not have to be either costly or difficult.

The major uses to which different types of neglected and derelict land can be put are given in Table 7.1. The opportunities are remarkable and leave little excuse not to restore except on grounds of expense.

Different types of restoration cost different amounts. High grade treatments applied to difficult sites are bound to cost a great deal. Simpler treatments to achieve less demanding end uses can be much cheaper, e.g. wildlife and amenity use (Table 7.2). Obviously, it is not desirable to

Table 7.1 Uses for different types of waste land

Old use	New use								
	Agriculture	Forestry	Housing	Industry	Amenity	Sport	Water sport	Nature conservation	Waste disposal
Neglected land	★★	★	★	★	★	★	?	★	★
Dry pit	★★	★	★	★	★	★		★★	★★
Wet pit			★		★		★★	★★	
Mine waste	★	★	?	?	★	★		★	★
Refuse tip	★				★★	★★		★	★
Housing			★★	★★	★★	★			★
Industry			?	★★	★	★		★	★

★★ the most likely new use
★ possible new use
? possible new use depending on circumstance

convert all derelict land to these ends but a low cost treatment, while it may not be the best solution, does not prejudice a final, more elaborate, solution. It will remove the immediate problem and it may be able to provide a temporary, yet commercially profitable, operation such as grass cropping. Meanwhile the land is in a land bank, improving under the influence of natural processes. There is great need for us to develop imagination and flexibility in land restoration.

Table 7.2 Some costs of different types of land restoration by the Greater Manchester and Lancashire joint reclamation team (excluding site acquisition and staff costs)

		costs per hectare (£)
1.	Agriculture after regrading without imported soil	
	Chisnall Hall (73.8ha)	7,350
	Hart Common (12.6ha)	16,025
	Rowley (14.4ha)	21,765
	Higher Folds (190.4ha)	16,335
2.	Extra cost of imported top soil 15cm depth	12,000
3.	Tree planting after regrading	
	Welch Whittle (13.2ha)	20,395
	Ladyshore (12.3ha)	8,250
4.	Tree planting without regrading	
	notch planting	1,325
	pit planting	2,550
5.	Very limited improvement to enhance colonisation	
	Nob End (9.5ha)	725
		(1983 prices)

Transforming our Waste Land: The Way Forward

Figure 7.1 A simple low cost treatment of a temporarily cleared area, designed to require minimum maintenance.

No matter what is done, there are important benefits to set against the restoration costs. A complete formal cost/benefit analysis of derelict land restoration is difficult and has rarely been attempted. However Table 7.3 illustrates three hypothetical examples of restoration and gives their estimated costs. The many positive benefits to be obtained from restoration certainly argue that an effective way forward must be found.

Table 7.3 The benefits of restoration set against their likely costs.

NEGATIVE QUALITIES TO BE REMOVED	→	COSTS	→	POSITIVE QUALITIES TO BE GAINED

Example 1 Urban clearance area to amenity until redevelopment (0.4ha) – informal open space surrounded by trees and shrubs

NEGATIVE QUALITIES TO BE REMOVED	COSTS	POSITIVE QUALITIES TO BE GAINED
Reduction of local morale	Site clearance	Encouragement of developers
Attraction of fly tipping	Seeding grass without top soil	Creation of safe recreation and play area
Movement of materials onto roadways	Planting shrubs	Raising self esteem of local population
Ammunition for vandals	Paths	
Negative effect on potential developers of area	Fencing	Attractive paths for pedestrians
		Habitat for wild life
Total	£6,000 (£1.5 per m²)	

Example 2 Colliery spoil heaps to agriculture (50ha) and housing (10ha) – grassland without topsoil and some trees

Visual impact on countryside	Earth moving	Gain of productive agricultural land
Source of eroded material to stream	Drainage	Improvement of landscape
Attraction of fly tipping	Cultivation & fertilising & seeding	Habitat for wild life
Reduction of local morale	Fencing	Maintenance by tenant
Source of danger	Preparation for housing	Rental income
		Profit on sale of land for housing
Total	£1.2million (£20,000 per ha)	

Example 3 Sand and gravel pit to recreation and wild life (30ha) – open water, clubhouse and visitor centre, and wilderness area

Attraction of fly tipping	Removal of rubbish and tidying margins	Provision of important recreation facility
Source of danger		Development of wild life habitat
Visual impact on neighbourhood	Planting wilderness area using voluntary labour	Provision of educational facility
		Improvement of landscape
	Boat ramp and hard standing	Rental income
	Clubhouse	Improved security of area
	Restoration of boundaries and roads	
Total	£300,000 (£10,000 per ha)	

7.2 How to deal with the past

The heritage of degraded land from the past is inescapable. The present size of the problem is clear, but the fact that new derelict land will continue to form, largely because of the unforeseen collapse of individual activities, must also be accepted.

Finance

The first problem to solve is that of economics – finding the money with which to carry out the desired restoration plans. Wherever possible, it is to be hoped that the previous owner, as in the case of the Tate and Lyle site in Liverpool, will contribute substantially. But alas this cannot always be the case. As a result, government grants, through the Derelict Land Act 1982,, are high on the list of sources of support and will clearly have to remain so. Schemes, designed to bring about private sector after-use, are very important, since the restored land is assured of a subsequent use and is not then a liability for the local authority. It is to be hoped in the future that more money will be available to private owners and developers. Financial support is also available in indirect ways from the government through special grants for particular purposes, such as forestry and sport. Charitable organisations must continue to have an important part to play in small and local projects, especially where there is a high level of community involvement.

Derelict and neglected land, once restored, has a value. If the restoration is both sensitive and imaginative, the value can be considerably greater than the original. It is therefore crucial that all would-be developers see and understand this. Some certainly do. The full development potential of every derelict site must be achieved, not necessarily by some grandiose scheme out of keeping with the surrounding area, but by a scheme which is sensible and yet creative. Interim uses, such as waste disposal, can clearly help in this.

There will, however, always be sites for which it is difficult to find money for restoration. There are a whole range of low cost solutions which should be more widely used. Some of our most valued open space, such as the upper part of Hampstead Heath in London, are the result of doing almost nothing to what was once derelict land. As we finish dealing with the most difficult sites, those that remain can very readily be treated by low cost techniques.

Many people involved in land reclamation, particularly those in local government, feel that the most important problem is not finding the capital to carry out the restoration but the revenue to maintain it afterwards. As a result, some local authorities, already extremely short of revenue, are not able to extend their areas of restored land. This is understandable but is a negative position. Perhaps the need is for more revenue and less capital. But the first solution to the problem at the

Figure 7.2   In the middle of the last century the top of Hampstead Heath was a vast sandpit; with almost no treatment it has become a beautiful and popular wilderness; an 1867 photograph of the land beside the road to the Spaniards Inn and the same site today.

Figure 7.3 An end use such as grass cropping can pay for maintenance.

moment must be to rethink both the land-use and the design of restored areas. Wherever possible a beneficial end-use should be chosen, such as some form of agriculture or horticulture or sport, which actually earns for the area its own maintenance. In urban clearance areas, for instance, allotments, although they may be fairly expensive to establish, require no local authority maintenance subsequently. Where this is not possible then a design should be chosen which requires only very low maintenance. In this respect organised wilderness, such as Hampstead Heath and the recent remarkable wild gardens of the International Garden Festival, are very possible and important solutions.

An alternative solution to the problem of maintenance costs if no extra revenue is available, is to pass the land over from the local authority to someone or some organisation who can develop and maintain it. Here attitudes need to change. It is no use any organisation being 'dog in the manger'. Local authorities have a long involvement in land reclamation and it is unfortunately true that a large proportion of neglected and badly maintained land is held by them. It is high time, as is happening in some urban areas, that local authorities collaborate with developers (for instance, in housing) to get these areas back into use. There is often a problem, however, because the local authority may have acquired the land at a high price, hoping to sell it for a profit after reclamation. This may not be possible and has created a serious situation needing immediate attention.

Organisations
The dominant organisations in land restoration in the past have been local authorities, because they have been the only bodies to receive Government grants. They must continue to shoulder their responsibility as the local organisations set up to work on our behalf. All public money is in short supply, but this does not stop local authorities working towards the solution of our outstanding derelict land problems. It is unfortunate that local authorities have to try to fit land restoration into the annual accounts procedure which dogs all public expenditure. Many have realised the value of having a 'rolling' programme which enables work to be started just as soon as the opportunity becomes available.

In some areas local authorities have the support of Groundwork Trusts set up in collaboration with the Countryside Commission and central Government. These are enabling money to be focussed onto smaller schemes and onto areas of neglected rather than derelict land. Groundwork Trusts are also an important way to achieve collaboration over restoration with industry and the general public. The Groundwork Trusts are being extended to new areas and are an important way forward, but they have to become self-supporting.

Industries and individuals have a very considerable part to play, not only as landowners but also as potential land developers. Industries should be prepared to contribute from their own resources, but there are opportunities, assisted by the different sources of financial support discussed in Chapter 4, that can be of direct benefit. Individuals must not be forgotten because they have the power to see things more creatively than corporations and can be more single-minded in achieving their goals. They have a considerable role to play in the future.

Finally, there are local and specialist groups which are united in relation to a particular interest, whether it is their play group, their school, their parish, their sport, amenity or nature conservation. This can include national bodies such as the Royal Society for the Protection of Birds and the Nature Conservancy Council. Over the years their singleminded concern has done much to preserve and nurture areas in both town and countryside. Part of the problem of derelict land can become their asset; many local nature reserves were once quarries and several sailing clubs

Figure 7.4 A sailing club adopts a flooded gravel pit; Papercourt, Surrey.

utilise flooded gravel pits. They should be encouraged and helped to seek out sites that can be developed for their purposes, particularly because when they assume responsibility for the site, it is no longer a liability to local authorities. They often have enthusiasm but little skill as developers, and organisations set up to help them, such as COMTECHSA (Community Technical Services Agency) in Liverpool (see Figure 4.4), and Groundwork Trusts, are very valuable.

Planning
Derelict and neglected land is land which has escaped proper planning, and planning cannot be retrospective. Nevertheless the planning process can exert, indirectly, considerable pressure on this inheritance. Where adequate urban sites are available, there is no need to allow green field developments. At the same time, planning officers can guide their councils into systematic programmes of urban restoration. Older areas in cities can be restructured and thereby attract the business and development which is otherwise looking for green field sites. People in the area will, hopefully, then have a greater pride in their surroundings, danger and ugliness can be removed, and good agricultural land can be saved from unnecessary sterilisation beneath buildings.

7.3 How can we prevent waste land in the future?

Dereliction can be prevented in the future. There is a strong tradition in this country which shows that the key to a wise land use lies in intelligent forward planning. Present legislation already requires that applications for mineral workings have to be accompanied by adequate and practical restoration plans for both the immediate future and the long term. Planning officers already look further into the future of sites before permission is given to develop them. This must continue and become necessary for all types of site and land use. Progressive restoration must also be required wherever possible so that the minimum amount of land remains untreated at any one time.

Industry and other users of land must realise their responsibilities. It seems a terrible indictment on us all if users of land only act when prompted by planners. They can and should do what is required to preserve our land heritage without pressure. After all, we all stand to gain or lose by what is done or not done.

Figure 7.5 Public bodies must set a good example in all their workings. Tidy operational land at Cortonwood Colliery, Barnsley; a grassed bank hides the operation from nearby housing.

Ways must be found to extend restoration to active sites for which there is no present restoration requirement. There are still about 16,000 hectares of these. Obviously such a move cannot take place at a stroke, but must be the result of initiatives by planning authorities and industries, to achieve an effective restoration on the basis of the 'best practicable means' by which the land may be returned to some new use. It is to be hoped that planners will encourage voluntary agreements to this end.

It is commonly believed that in all mining and other developments we should expect restoration to mean restoration in the narrow sense, replacing exactly what was there before. This seems a rather restrictive expectation. It is obvious that the area of agricultural land should not be diminished, but there are situations where restoration would be excessively difficult and place an unreasonable demand on the industry. It is more sensible to ensure, with the benefit of imagination and experience, that the final land use in these cases is generally beneficial, as has already been argued for areas derived from past dereliction.

A beneficial end use is the crucial criterion, since land may fall back into decline if it is uneconomic after restoration. In areas where an agricultural end use is not really practical, then forestry, amenity or even a hard land use, may be excellent alternative solutions. Wild areas are another solution because of their low capital and maintenance costs. For any site the whole range of alternatives should be explored, in relation, of course, to the nature of the site and its surroundings.

Planning officers, because of their special knowledge of the local problems, also have a particular responsibility to guide and lead local programmes in collaboration with their council. A great deal can be done if the public as a whole is not only kept informed but also brought into collaborative relationship. After all, it is our joint problem.

Future dereliction must also be discouraged by the setting of good examples of land management by local authorities in the land they own, by the encouragement of public bodies and industries, great and small, to interest themselves in the appearance of their property, by good relationships with the minerals industry, and by interesting the public in creative land restoration schemes.

Local authorities, because they are responsible not only for planning but also for development and management of many sites on our behalf, should realise that they are in a very sensitive position because they are both poacher and gamekeeper. It would be pleasant to believe that their standards of management were always of the highest calibre, but they are not.

At the same time, the actual quality of future land restoration must be more carefully monitored than it has been in the past. There is no point in carrying out restoration if regular checks are not made to ensure that the desired end use is achieved. Planning authorities often fail to inspect carefully enough the restoration they have required as a planning condition, and developers then discover where they can cut corners. For agricultural restoration, development of soil structure and site productivity needs to be followed over a number of years, to establish whether longer term improvements have been achieved. Some developers are beginning to do this (see Case Study 6.8). There is a responsibility for standards in restoration which rests heavily on the shoulders of both the local authorities who have the control and of the developer who carries out the work.

7.4 Pooling of resources

The restoration of land is a multi-disciplinary operation, requiring input from experts in landscape, agriculture, soil science, forestry, ecology, hydrology and civil engineering, if a viable and cost-effective end product is to be achieved. To deal with both the past and the future, the formation and maintenance of specialist land reclamation teams in local government and in industry is crucial, and these teams must be prepared, wherever necessary, themselves to seek the expert advice of others.

Because of the progress in methods of restoration, there is a great need for the exchange of ideas, results and opinions between all the people

Figure 7.6 If we manage our land with imagination and care, we need not pass on wasteland to our children; this forest in a pleasant landscape in Durham was a bare colliery spoil tip 20 years ago.

involved. This does not mean just the planner, the academic research worker and the contractor in the field, but anyone who is involved in coping with the problem, whether in industry, local government or the general public. By this, methods of achieving success can be exchanged, and failures can be understood. Restoration methods in the recent past have been led by technology and finance. In the future they should also be guided by natural processes and community requirements. Creative ideas and innovations which are labour-saving and cheap should be communicated as widely as possible and not kept as private information. At the moment we have hardly begun this exchange.

It is probably true to say that most of the major organisations and disciplines who should be taking an active part in restoration projects are doing so. However, more ecologists, social scientists and local communities could, and should, be involved and consulted at the planning stage. But perhaps, in particular, local communities must be much more involved from the early planning to the final maintenance stage. We must think more clearly about our aims and objectives. In the end it is the needs of the community and the value of the environment which should guide us.

Our surroundings do not just happen. They are the result of the accumulated aspirations and effects of people over many centuries. In future we must choose to have the surroundings, the environment, that we are prepared to work for and even fight for. People in the past who have worked hard to give us, despite all its problems, this very attractive country of ours, would be dishonoured if we did not try to solve our present problems. More importantly, we should not let down those that will succeed us. The choice of what we do, and the success or failure which results, is ours alone.

Appendix I

Further Reading

The nature of the problem

Derelict Britain, J. Barr, Penguin Books, 1969.

Derelict Land, K. L. Wallwork, David and Charles, Newton Abbot, 1974.

Urban Wasteland, T. Cantell, Civic Trust, London, 1977.

The Endless Village, W. C. Teagle, Nature Conservancy Council, London, 1978.

Britain's Wasting Areas, G. Moss, Architectural Press, London, 1981.

Derelict and Waste Land: Britain's Neglected Land Resource, V. N. Dennington and M. J. Chadwick, Journal of Environmental Management **16**, 229-239, 1983.

Survey of Land for Mineral Working in England 1982. Department of the Environment, London, 1984.

Survey of Derelict Land in England 1982. Department of the Environment, 1984.

Ideas and methods for its solution

New Lives, New Landscapes, N. Fairbrother, Penguin Books, 1972.

Quarries and the Landscape, S. Hayward, British Quarrying and Slag Federation, London, 1974.

Environmental Impact of Mining, C. G. Down and J. Stocks, Applied Science Publishers, London 1977.

Colonisation of Industrial Wasteland, R. P. Gemmell, Edward Arnold, London, 1977.

The Restoration of Land, A. D. Bradshaw and M. J. Chadwick, Blackwell, Oxford, 1980.

Establishing Trees on Regraded Spoil Heaps, J. Jobling and F. Stevens, Forestry Commission, Farnham, 1980.

Countryside Management in the Urban Fringe, Countryside Commission, Cheltenham, 1981.

Towards Community Uses of Wasteland, J. Stearn, Wasteland Forum, London, 1981.

Land Reclamation in Cities, R. A. Dutton and A. D. Bradshaw, HMSO, London, 1982.

Mine Wastes Reclamation, N. A. Williamson, M. S. Johnson and A. D. Bradshaw, Mining Journal Books, London, 1982.

Quarry Reclamation, N. J. Coppin and A. D. Bradshaw, Mining Journal Books, London, 1982.

A Guide to Habitat Creation, Ecology Handbook No. 2, C. Baines and J. Smart, G.L.C. London, 1984.

Tackling Dereliction, T. Aldous, Federation of Civil Engineering Contractors, London, 1984.

EEC Environmental Policy and Britain, N. Haigh, Environmental Data Services, London, 1984.

Reclamation of Contaminated Land, M. A. Smith (ed), Plenum, NATO, 1985.

A Guide to the Reclamation of Mineral Workings for Forestry, K. Wilson, Forestry Commission, 1985.

Various Papers prepared by the Interdepartmental Committee on the Redevelopment of Contaminated Land (ICRCL):
Notes on the redevelopment of landfill sites – ICRCL, 17/78.
Notes on the development of gasworks sites – ICRCL, 18/79.
Notes on the redevelopment of sewage works and farms – ICRCL, 23/79.
Notes on the redevelopment of scrapyards and similar sites – ICRCL, 42/80.
Guidance on the assessment and redevelopment of contaminated land – ICRCL, 59/83.
Notes on the fire hazards of contaminated land – ICRCL, 61/84.

Appendix II

Sources of Advice

Planning and grant aid

District Planning Departments for general advice.

County Planning Departments for waste disposal, mineral working, land reclamation.

Regional Offices of the Department of the Environment for grant aid applications.

Engineering problems

Many firms; details from the Building Research Establishment, Garston, Herts. WD2 7JR.

Biological problems

Many specialists; details from Institute of Biology, 20 Queensferry Place, London SW7 2DZ.

Chemical analysis

County and District Public Analysts, Agricultural Development and Advisory Service, Ministry of Agriculture Fisheries and Food, Local analytic firms.

Landscape design

Many firms; details from Landscape Institute, 12 Carlton House Terrace, London SW1Y 5AH.

Contractors

Local firms; details from British Association of Landscape Industries, 7 Henry St., Keighley, W. Yorks BD21 3DR.

Specialists

Countryside Commission (recreation), Crescent Place, Cheltenham, GL50 3RA.

Forestry Commission (tree planting), Alice Holt, Wrecclesham, Farnham, Surrey GU10 4LH.

Ministry of Agriculture, Fisheries and Food (agriculture), local offices.

Nature Conservancy Council (nature conservation), Northminster House, Peterborough, PE1 1UA.

Sports Turf Research Institute (sports areas), Bingley, W. Yorks, BD16 1AU.

Local Trusts for Nature Conservation (conservation) details from the Royal Society for Nature Conservation, The Green, Nettleham, Lincoln, LN2 2NR.

Acknowledgements

We are very grateful for the unstinted help given by so many people. In particular, we would like to thank:

For case studies:
J. Barford (Gateshead Metropolitan District Council)
B. Calvert (Melbourne Wood Partnership)
T. Cramb (Durham County Council)
G. F. M. Dawe (Rural Preservation Association)
G. Doubleday (Durham County Council)
E. C. Dunn (West Midlands County Council)
T. Edwards (Brian Clouston and Partners)
R. P. Gemmel (Greater Manchester County Council)
C. F. J. Grigg (English China Clays)
J. F. Handley (Operation Groundwork)
C. H. Head (NCB Open Cast Executive)
G. D. R. Parry (University of Liverpool, EAU)
W. J. Spreull (St. Albans Sand and Gravel)
D. Thomas (Amey Roadstone Corporation)

For photographs:
R. M. Bell (University of Liverpool, EAU)
W. O. Binns (Forestry Commission)
C. J. C. Bradshaw (London)
E. Brent-Jones (NCB Open Cast Executive)
W. Brookes (Operation Groundwork)
R. N. Bryant (CEGB Generation Dev. Div.)
P. Bulmer (Operation Groundwork)
G. P. Challenger (Peak District National Park)
Mrs. A. Geoffrey (Forestry Commission)
J. Melton (Ready Mix Concrete)
P. Moullin (NCB Deep Mines Executive)
National Water Sports Centre (Nottingham)
M. O'Connor (Stoke-on-Trent City Council)
D. M. Parker (University of Liverpool, EAU)
P. D. Putwain (University of Liverpool, EAU)

J. Ritchie (Merseyside Development Corporation)
M. G. Tassell (Cambridgeshire County Council)
A. J. Tollitt (University of Liverpool, Department of Botany)

For drawings

S. J. Prescott (University of Liverpool, EAU)
Nature Conservancy Council (for Fig 2.10)

For additional views

N. Beard (Ministry of Agriculture, Fisheries and Food)
J. C. R. Bowman (Tarmac Roadstone)
M. J. Chadwick (University of York, Department of Biology)
D. Fourt (Forestry Commission)
I. Gilfoyle (Cheshire County Council)
P. E. Gawn (Amey Roadstone Corporation)
P. Jennins (E. H. Williams: Environment)
J. Jobling (Forestry Commission)
G. Luscombe (Rural Preservation Assoc)
R. Madders (Merseyside Task Force)
S. Matthews (Liverpool City Council)
R. N. Percival (Department of the Environment, N.W.)
M. A. Smith (Building Research Establishment)

We would also like to thank the many others who have helped us and returned questionnaires.

Finally we would like to thank Ann Ward (DoE) for her unstinting guidance and encouragement.

ALISON BURT
ANTHONY BRADSHAW

Printed in the U.K. for Her Majesty's Stationery Office
Dd 0738685   PS 5250509   1/86